Instant Pot®

COOKBOOK

pil

Publications International, Ltd.

Welcome to the wonderful world of Instant Pot® cooking! Although the current craze makes it seem like a new invention, pressure cooking has actually been around for a few hundred years. Many people grew up hearing stories of pressure cooker catastrophes—exploding pots and soup on the ceiling—but those days are long gone. There have been great changes and improvements in recent years to make modern pressure cookers completely safe, quiet and easy to use.

What makes the Instant Pot® different?

The Instant Pot® is a versatile electric multi-cooker that can be a pressure cooker, rice cooker, slow cooker, steamer and yogurt maker. The cooking programs you'll find on the control panel are convenient shortcuts for some foods you may prepare regularly (rice, beans, etc.) which use preset times and cooking levels. But in these pages we'll explore the basics of pressure cooking with recipes that primarily use the Manual or Pressure Cook button along with customized cooking times and pressure levels. These simple and delicious dishes will inspire you to use your Instant Pot® daily and create your own Instant Pot® magic!

Instant Pot® Cooking Basics

Every recipe is slightly different, but most include these basic steps. Read through the entire recipe before beginning to cook so you'll know what ingredients to add and when to add them, which pressure level to use, the cooking time and the release method.

1. Sauté: Many recipes call for sautéing vegetables or browning meat at the beginning of a recipe to add flavor. (Be sure to leave the lid off in this step.)

2. Add the ingredients as the recipe directs and secure the lid, making sure the arrow mark on the lid is aligned with the "close" mark and lock icon on the rim of the outside pot. Turn the pressure release valve to the Sealing position.

3. Select Manual or Pressure Cook, then choose the pressure level. The default setting is high pressure, which is what most recipes in this book use. To change to low pressure, use the Adjust or Pressure Level button. To set the cooking time, use the + and - buttons. The Instant Pot® will start automatically.

4. Once the pressure cooking is complete, use the pressure release method directed by the recipe. There are three types of releases:

Natural release: Let the pressure slowly release on its own, which can take anywhere from 5 to 25 minutes (but is typically in the 10- to 15-minute range). The release time will be shorter for a pot that is less full and longer for one that is more full. When the float valve lowers, the pressure is released and you can open the lid.

Quick release: Use a towel or pot holder to manually turn the pressure valve to the Venting position immediately after the cooking is complete. (Be sure to get out of the way of the steam before turning the valve.) It can take up to 2 minutes to fully release all the pressure; the float valve will drop down when all the pressure is released.

A combination of natural and quick release: The recipe will instruct you to let the pressure release naturally for a certain amount of time (frequently for 10 minutes), and then do a quick release as directed.

Tips, Tricks, Dos and Don'ts

- Read the manual before beginning. There may be features you won't use, but it will eliminate some beginner's confusion, and it can help you understand how the Instant Pot® works—and see all its possibilities. Models also change over time, so the manual can provide the best information about the buttons and functions of your pot. (Note that the terms "Manual" and "Pressure Cook" are interchangeable.)

- Don't overfill the pot—the total amount of food and liquid should not exceed the maximum level marked on the inner pot. Generally it is best not to fill the pot more than two thirds full; when cooking foods that expand during cooking such as beans and grains, do not fill it more than half full.

- Make sure there is always some liquid in the pot before cooking because a minimum amount is required to come up to pressure (the amount differs between models). However, if the recipe contains a large quantity of vegetables or meats, you may be able to use a bit less since these ingredients will create their own liquid.)

- Always check that the pressure release valve is in the right position before you start pressure cooking. The food simply won't get cooked if the valve is not in the Sealing position because there will not be enough pressure in the pot.

- Never try to force the lid open after cooking—if the lid won't open, that means the pressure has not fully released. (As a safety feature, the lid remains locked until the float valve drops down.)

- Save the thickeners for after the pressure cooking is done. Pressure cooker recipes often end up with a lot of flavorful liquid left in the pot when cooking is complete; flour or cornstarch mixtures can thicken these liquids into delicious sauces. Use the Sauté function while incorporating the thickeners into the cooking liquid, and then cook and stir until the desired consistency is reached.

- Keep in mind that cooking times in some recipes may vary. We've included pressure cooking time charts as a guide (pages 212—215), but these are approximate times, and numerous variables may cause your results to be different. For example, the freshness of dried beans affects their cooking time (older beans take longer to cook), as does what they are cooked with—hard water (water that is high in mineral content), acidic ingredients, sugar and salt levels can also affect cooking times. So be flexible and experiment with what works best for you—you can always check the doneness of your food and add more time.

- Set reasonable expectations, i.e., don't expect everything you cook in the pressure cooker to be ready in a few minutes. Even though it reduces many conventional cooking times dramatically, nothing is literally "instant"—it will always take time to get up to pressure, and then to release it. (These machines are fast but not magical!)

Chili Verde *(page 42)*

Mole Chili *(page 34)*

Pressure Cooker Meat Loaf *(page 10)*

BEEF, PORK & LAMB

Maple Spice
Rubbed Ribs
(page 52)

Braised Chipotle Beef *(page 12)*

Beer Barbecued
Pulled Pork Sandwiches
(page 40)

Spicy-Sweet
Lamb Tagine
(page 54)

BEEF, PORK & LAMB

2 tablespoons vegetable oil

3 pounds bone-in beef short ribs, trimmed and cut into 3-inch pieces

1 teaspoon Italian seasoning

¾ teaspoon salt

¼ teaspoon black pepper

1½ cups chopped leeks (2 to 3 leeks)

½ cup dry white wine

¾ cup pitted kalamata or oil-cured olives

1¼ cups prepared pasta sauce

Parmesan Polenta (recipe follows, optional)

1. Press Sauté; heat oil in Instant Pot®. Add short ribs in batches; cook about 8 minutes or until browned on all sides. Remove to plate; season with Italian seasoning, salt and pepper. Drain off all but 1 tablespoon fat.

2. Add leeks to pot; cook and stir 2 minutes or until softened. Add wine; cook until almost evaporated, scraping up browned bits from bottom of pot. Return short ribs to pot with olives; pour pasta sauce over short ribs.

3. Secure lid and move pressure release valve to Sealing position. Press Manual; cook at high pressure 30 minutes.

4. When cooking is complete, use natural release for 10 minutes, then release remaining pressure. Meanwhile, prepare Parmesan Polenta, if desired. Serve ribs and sauce with polenta.

MAKES 4 SERVINGS

PARMESAN POLENTA: Bring 2 cups water to a boil in large nonstick saucepan. Gradually whisk in 1 cup instant polenta until smooth and thick. Stir in ½ cup grated Parmesan cheese. Season with salt and pepper.

CORNED BEEF AND CABBAGE

1 corned beef brisket
    (3 to 4 pounds) with
    seasoning packet

2 cups water

1 head cabbage
    (1½ pounds), cut
    into 6 wedges

1 package (16 ounces)
    baby carrots

1. Place corned beef in Instant Pot®, fat side up; sprinkle with seasoning. Pour water into pot.

2. Secure lid and move pressure release valve to Sealing position. Press Manual; cook at high pressure 90 minutes.

3. When cooking is complete, use natural release for 10 minutes, then release remaining pressure. Remove beef to cutting board; tent with foil.

4. Add cabbage and carrots to pot. Secure lid and move pressure release valve to Sealing position. Press Manual; cook at high pressure 4 minutes. When cooking is complete, press Cancel and use quick release.

5. Slice beef; serve with vegetables.

MAKES 3 TO 4 SERVINGS

ESPRESSO-LACED POT ROAST

1 tablespoon packed
brown sugar

1 tablespoon
espresso powder

1½ teaspoons salt,
divided

1 teaspoon black
pepper, divided

1 boneless beef
chuck roast
(2 to 2½ pounds)

1½ tablespoons
vegetable oil

1 large onion,
chopped

1 cup beef broth

½ teaspoon dried
thyme

2 bay leaves

6 to 8 red potatoes
(about 2 pounds),
peeled and cut
into 1-inch pieces

1 pound carrots, cut
into 1-inch pieces

3 tablespoons water

2 tablespoons all-
purpose flour

Chopped fresh
parsley (optional)

1. Combine brown sugar, espresso powder, ½ teaspoon salt and ½ teaspoon pepper in small bowl; mix well. Rub mixture into all sides of beef.

2. Press Sauté; heat oil in Instant Pot®. Add beef; cook about 6 minutes or until browned on all sides. Remove to plate. Add onion to pot; cook and stir 3 minutes or until softened. Add broth, thyme, bay leaves, remaining 1 teaspoon salt and ½ teaspoon pepper; cook and stir 2 minutes, scraping up browned bits from bottom of pot. Return beef to pot.

3. Secure lid and move pressure release valve to Sealing position. Press Manual; cook at high pressure 60 minutes.

4. When cooking is complete, press Cancel and use quick release. Add potatoes and carrots to pot, pressing vegetables into cooking liquid. Secure lid and move pressure release valve to Sealing position. Press Manual; cook at high pressure 4 minutes.

5. When cooking is complete, press Cancel and use quick release. Remove beef and vegetables to platter; tent with foil. Remove and discard bay leaves.

6. Stir water into flour in small bowl until smooth. Press Sauté. Add flour mixture to sauce; cook about 5 minutes or until sauce is reduced and thickens, stirring frequently. Serve sauce with beef and vegetables; garnish with parsley.

MAKES 4 TO 6 SERVINGS

PRESSURE COOKER MEAT LOAF

1 tablespoon olive oil

1 small onion, finely chopped

½ red bell pepper, finely chopped

3 cloves garlic, minced

1 teaspoon dried oregano

1½ cups water

2 pounds ground meat loaf mix *or* 1 pound each ground beef and ground pork

1 egg

3 tablespoons tomato paste

1 teaspoon salt

½ teaspoon black pepper

1. Press Sauté; heat oil in Instant Pot®. Add onion, bell pepper, garlic and oregano; cook and stir 3 minutes or until vegetables are softened. Remove to large bowl; let cool 5 minutes. Wipe out pot with paper towels; add water and rack to pot.

2. Add meat loaf mix, egg, tomato paste, salt and black pepper to vegetable mixture; mix well. Tear off 18×12-inch piece of foil; fold in half crosswise to create 12×9-inch rectangle. Shape meat mixture into 7×5-inch oval on foil; bring up sides of foil to create pan, leaving top of meat loaf uncovered. Place foil with meat loaf on rack in pot.

3. Secure lid and move pressure release valve to Sealing position. Press Manual; cook at high pressure 37 minutes.

4. When cooking is complete, press Cancel and use quick release. Remove meat loaf to cutting board; let stand 10 minutes before slicing.

MAKES 6 SERVINGS

SWEET AND SAVORY BRISKET

1 teaspoon salt, divided

½ teaspoon black pepper

1 small beef brisket (2½ to 3 pounds), trimmed

1 large onion, thinly sliced

½ cup beef or chicken broth

⅓ cup chili sauce

1 tablespoon packed brown sugar

½ teaspoon dried thyme

¼ teaspoon ground cinnamon

2 large sweet potatoes, peeled and cut into 1-inch pieces

1 cup pitted prunes

¼ cup water

2 tablespoons cornstarch

1. Rub ½ teaspoon salt and pepper into all surfaces of beef. Place beef in Instant Pot®; top with onion. Combine broth, chili sauce, brown sugar, thyme, cinnamon and remaining ½ teaspoon salt in small bowl; mix well. Pour over beef and onion.

2. Secure lid and move pressure release valve to Sealing position. Press Manual; cook at high pressure 70 minutes.

3. When cooking is complete, use natural release for 10 minutes, then release remaining pressure. Remove beef to cutting board; tent with foil.

4. Add sweet potatoes and prunes to pot. Press Manual; cook at high pressure 3 minutes. When cooking is complete, press Cancel and use quick release. Remove vegetables to bowl with slotted spoon.

5. Stir water into cornstarch in small bowl until smooth. Press Sauté. Add cornstarch mixture to pot; cook and stir 1 to 2 minutes or until sauce thickens.

6. Cut brisket into thin slices across the grain. Serve with sweet potato mixture and sauce.

MAKES 4 SERVINGS

BRAISED CHIPOTLE BEEF

3 pounds boneless beef chuck roast, cut into 1-inch pieces

2 teaspoons salt, divided

¾ teaspoon black pepper, divided

3 tablespoons vegetable oil, divided

1 large onion, cut into 1-inch pieces

2 red bell peppers, cut into 1½-inch pieces

3 tablespoons tomato paste

1 tablespoon minced garlic

1 tablespoon chipotle chili powder

1 tablespoon paprika

1 tablespoon ground cumin

1 teaspoon dried oregano

¼ cup water

1 can (about 14 ounces) diced tomatoes

Hot cooked rice or tortillas (optional)

1. Pat beef dry with paper towels; season with ½ teaspoon salt and ¼ teaspoon black pepper.

2. Press Sauté; heat 2 tablespoons oil in Instant Pot®. Add beef in two batches; cook about 5 minutes or until browned. Remove to plate.

3. Heat remaining 1 tablespoon oil in pot. Add onion; cook and stir 3 minutes or until softened. Add bell peppers; cook and stir 2 minutes. Add tomato paste, garlic, chili powder, paprika, cumin, oregano, remaining 1½ teaspoons salt and ½ teaspoon black pepper; cook and stir 1 minute. Stir in water, scraping up browned bits from bottom of pot. Return beef to pot with tomatoes; mix well.

4. Secure lid and move pressure release valve to Sealing position. Press Manual; cook at high pressure 30 minutes.

5. When cooking is complete, use natural release for 10 minutes, then release remaining pressure. Serve with rice or tortillas, if desired.

MAKES 4 TO 6 SERVINGS

SERVING SUGGESTIONS: Add rice and/or beans to the beef and use it as a filling for tacos or burritos. Or serve over mashed potatoes.

2 cloves garlic, minced

1 teaspoon salt

1 teaspoon herbes de Provence*

1 teaspoon ground sage

1 teaspoon ground cumin

1 teaspoon black pepper

1 beef eye of round roast (about 2½ pounds), well trimmed

2 tablespoons olive oil

1 cup beef broth

4 small turnips, peeled and cut into wedges

12 medium fresh brussels sprouts, trimmed

2 cups halved small new red potatoes

2 cups baby carrots

1 cup pearl onions, skins removed *or* 1 large onion, cut into wedges

*Or substitute ¼ teaspoon each dried rosemary, thyme, sage and savory.

1. Combine garlic, salt, herbes de Provence, sage, cumin and pepper in small bowl; mix well. Rub mixture into all sides of beef.

2. Press Sauté; heat oil in Instant Pot®. Add beef; cook about 5 minutes or until browned. Remove to plate. Stir in broth, scraping up browned bits from bottom of pot. Place rack in pot; place beef on rack.

3. Secure lid and move pressure release valve to Sealing position. Press Manual; cook at high pressure 50 minutes.

4. When cooking is complete, use natural release for 5 minutes, then release remaining pressure.

5. Add turnips, brussels sprouts, potatoes, carrots and onions. Secure lid and move pressure release valve to Sealing position. Press Manual; cook at high pressure 10 minutes.

6. When cooking is complete, press Cancel and use quick release. Serve beef and vegetables with cooking liquid or thicken sauce, if desired.

MAKES 4 TO 6 SERVINGS

SHREDDED BEEF FAJITAS

1 beef flank steak
   (about 1 pound),
   cut into 2 pieces

¼ teaspoon salt

⅛ teaspoon black pepper

1 tablespoon vegetable oil

1 medium onion, chopped,
   divided

1 medium green bell
   pepper, cut into
   ½-inch pieces, divided

1 clove garlic, minced
   or ¼ teaspoon garlic
   powder

1 can (about 10 ounces)
   diced tomatoes with
   mild green chiles

½ package fajita
   seasoning mix
   (about 2 tablespoons)

6 (8-inch) flour tortillas

   Optional toppings:
   sour cream, guacamole,
   shredded Cheddar
   cheese, salsa

1. Season beef with salt and black pepper. Press Sauté; heat oil in Instant Pot®. Add beef; cook 3 to 4 minutes per side or until browned. Remove to plate. Add half of onion and half of bell pepper to pot; cook and stir 2 minutes. Add garlic; cook and stir 30 seconds. Add tomatoes and fajita seasoning mix; cook 2 minutes, scraping up browned bits from bottom of pot. Return beef to pot, pressing into liquid.

2. Secure lid and move pressure release valve to Sealing position. Press Manual; cook at high pressure 23 minutes.

3. When cooking is complete, use natural release for 10 minutes, then release remaining pressure. Remove beef to clean plate; let stand 10 minutes.

4. Meanwhile, press Sauté; add remaining half of onion and bell pepper to pot. Cook about 8 minutes or until bell pepper is crisp-tender and liquid is reduced, stirring occasionally.

5. Shred beef into bite-size pieces; return to pot and stir until blended. Serve beef mixture in tortillas with desired toppings.

MAKES 6 SERVINGS

EASY MEATBALLS

1 pound ground beef

1 egg, beaten

3 tablespoons Italian-seasoned dry bread crumbs

1 clove garlic, minced

1 teaspoon dried oregano

¾ teaspoon salt

¼ teaspoon black pepper

⅛ teaspoon ground red pepper

3 cups marinara or tomato-basil pasta sauce

Hot cooked spaghetti

Chopped fresh basil (optional)

Grated Parmesan cheese (optional)

1. Combine beef, egg, bread crumbs, garlic, oregano, salt, black pepper and red pepper in medium bowl; mix gently. Shape into 16 (1½-inch) meatballs.

2. Pour pasta sauce into Instant Pot®. Add meatballs to sauce; turn to coat and submerge meatballs in sauce.

3. Secure lid and move pressure release valve to Sealing position. Press Manual; cook at high pressure 8 minutes.

4. When cooking is complete, press Cancel and use quick release. Serve meatballs and sauce over spaghetti; top with basil and cheese, if desired.

MAKES 4 SERVINGS

TRADITIONAL GOULASH

⅓ cup all-purpose flour

2½ teaspoons salt, divided

1 teaspoon black pepper

2 pounds boneless beef chuck shoulder, cut into bite-size pieces

3 tablespoons vegetable oil, divided

2 shallots *or* 1 medium onion, finely chopped

3 cloves garlic, minced

1 can (28 ounces) diced tomatoes

1 tablespoon paprika (preferably Hungarian)

2 tablespoons chopped fresh parsley *or* 1 teaspoon dried parsley flakes

1 teaspoon dried thyme

2 bay leaves

¼ cup sour cream, or to taste

Hot cooked egg noodles

Chopped fresh dill (optional)

1. Combine flour, 2 teaspoons salt and pepper in large resealable food storage bag. Add beef; toss to coat. Shake off any excess flour mixture.

2. Press Sauté; heat 2 tablespoons oil in Instant Pot®. Add beef in two batches; cook about 5 minutes or until browned. Remove to plate.

3. Heat remaining 1 tablespoon oil in pot. Add shallots and garlic; cook and stir 2 minutes or until softened. Add tomatoes and paprika; cook and stir 2 minutes, scraping up browned bits from bottom of pot. Return beef and any juices to pot with parsley, thyme, bay leaves and remaining ½ teaspoon salt; mix well.

4. Secure lid and move pressure release valve to Sealing position. Press Manual; cook at high pressure 35 minutes.

5. When cooking is complete, use natural release for 10 minutes, then release remaining pressure.

6. Press Sauté; cook 5 minutes or until stew thickens slightly. Press Cancel; remove and discard bay leaves. Stir in sour cream until blended. Serve over noodles; garnish with dill.

MAKES 4 TO 6 SERVINGS

GREEK BEEF STEW

¼ cup all-purpose flour

2 teaspoons Greek seasoning

¼ teaspoon salt

¼ teaspoon black pepper

2 pounds bottom round or boneless beef chuck roast, cut into 1-inch pieces

2 tablespoons olive oil

½ cup beef broth

¼ cup tomato paste

1 pint grape or cherry tomatoes, divided

2 medium onions, each cut into 8 wedges

1 cup pitted kalamata olives

4 sprigs fresh oregano, plus additional for garnish

1 lemon, divided

1. Combine flour, Greek seasoning, salt and pepper in large resealable food storage bag. Add beef; toss to coat. Shake off any excess flour mixture. Press Sauté; heat oil in Instant Pot®. Add beef in two batches; cook about 5 minutes or until browned. Remove to plate. Add broth and tomato paste to pot; cook and stir 2 minutes, scraping up browned bits from bottom of pot. Stir in beef, ½ cup grape tomatoes, onions, olives, 4 sprigs oregano and juice of ½ lemon; mix well.

2. Secure lid and move pressure release valve to Sealing position. Press Manual; cook at high pressure 20 minutes.

3. When cooking is complete, use natural release for 10 minutes, then release remaining pressure.

4. Press Sauté; add remaining grape tomatoes to pot. Cook about 5 minutes or until tomatoes have softened and stew thickens, stirring frequently. Cut remaining ½ lemon into wedges; serve with stew. Garnish with additional oregano.

MAKES 4 TO 6 SERVINGS

BRISKET WITH VEGETABLES

1 tablespoon vegetable oil

1 beef brisket (4 to 5 pounds), well trimmed

2 onions, thinly sliced

4 cloves garlic, minced

2 teaspoons dried thyme

½ teaspoon ground coriander

1 cup beef broth

1 teaspoon salt

½ teaspoon black pepper

2 pounds red potatoes, quartered

1 pound baby carrots

3 tablespoons water

2 tablespoons all-purpose flour

1. Press Sauté; heat oil in Instant Pot®. Add brisket; cook until browned on all sides. Remove to plate. Add onions to pot; cook and stir 3 minutes or until softened. Add garlic, thyme and coriander; cook and stir 1 minute. Add broth, salt and pepper; cook and stir 1 minute, scraping up browned bits from bottom of pot. Return brisket to pot.

2. Secure lid and move pressure release valve to Sealing position. Press Manual; cook at high pressure 60 minutes.

3. When cooking is complete, use natural release for 10 minutes, then release remaining pressure.

4. Add potatoes and carrots to pot. Secure lid and move pressure release valve to Sealing position. Press Manual; cook at high pressure 10 minutes. When cooking is complete, use natural release for 10 minutes, then release remaining pressure. Remove brisket and vegetables to platter; cover loosely to keep warm.

5. Stir water into flour in small bowl until smooth. Add ¼ cup hot cooking liquid; stir until blended. Press Sauté; add flour mixture to remaining cooking liquid in pot. Cook and stir 3 to 4 minutes or until sauce thickens.

6. Slice brisket across the grain. Serve brisket and vegetables with sauce.

MAKES 8 SERVINGS

BACON AND STOUT SHORT RIBS

6 slices thick-cut bacon, chopped

4 pounds bone-in beef short ribs, trimmed and cut into 3-inch pieces

1 teaspoon salt, divided

½ teaspoon black pepper

1 large onion, cut in half and thinly sliced

1 tablespoon tomato paste

1 bottle or can (12 ounces) stout, dark beer or ale

2 tablespoons spicy brown mustard

1 bay leaf

3 tablespoons water

2 tablespoons all-purpose flour

2 tablespoons finely chopped fresh parsley

Hot mashed potatoes or cooked egg noodles (optional)

1. Press Sauté; cook bacon in Instant Pot® until crisp. Remove to paper towel-lined plate. Drain off all but 1 tablespoon drippings.

2. Season short ribs with ½ teaspoon salt and pepper. Add short ribs to pot in batches; cook about 8 minutes or until browned on all sides. Remove to plate. Drain off all but 1 tablespoon fat.

3. Add onion to pot; cook and stir 5 minutes or until golden brown. Add tomato paste; cook and stir 1 minute. Add stout, mustard, bay leaf and remaining ½ teaspoon salt; cook and stir 1 minute, scraping up browned bits from bottom of pot. Return bacon and short ribs to pot.

4. Secure lid and move pressure release valve to Sealing position. Press Manual; cook at high pressure 45 minutes.

5. When cooking is complete, use natural release for 10 minutes, then release remaining pressure. Remove short ribs to clean plate; tent with foil. Remove and discard bay leaf.

6. Skim excess fat from surface of sauce. Stir water into flour in small bowl until smooth. Press Sauté; add flour mixture to cooking liquid in pot, stirring constantly. Cook and stir sauce about 5 minutes or until thickened. Stir in parsley. Serve sauce with short ribs and mashed potatoes, if desired.

MAKES 4 TO 6 SERVINGS

SHORTCUT BOLOGNESE

1 tablespoon olive oil

1 pound ground beef

1 medium onion, chopped

½ small carrot, finely chopped

½ stalk celery, finely chopped

3 tablespoons tomato paste

1 cup dry white wine

½ cup milk

⅛ teaspoon ground nutmeg

1 can (about 14 ounces) whole tomatoes, coarsely chopped, juice reserved

½ cup beef broth

1 teaspoon salt

1 teaspoon dried basil

½ teaspoon dried thyme

⅛ teaspoon black pepper

1 bay leaf

Hot cooked spaghetti

Grated Parmesan cheese (optional)

1. Press Sauté; heat oil in Instant Pot®. Add beef; cook about 8 minutes or until all liquid evaporates, stirring to break up meat. Drain fat.

2. Add onion, carrot and celery to pot; cook and stir 4 minutes. Add tomato paste; cook and stir 2 minutes. Add wine; cook about 5 minutes or until wine has almost evaporated. Add milk and nutmeg; cook and stir 3 to 4 minutes or until milk has almost evaporated. Stir in tomatoes with juice, broth, salt, basil, thyme, pepper and bay leaf; mix well.

3. Secure lid and move pressure release valve to Sealing position. Press Manual; cook at high pressure 18 minutes.

4. When cooking is complete, press Cancel and use quick release. Remove and discard bay leaf. Serve sauce with spaghetti; top with cheese, if desired.

MAKES 4 SERVINGS

4 slices bacon, chopped

⅓ cup all-purpose flour

1½ teaspoons salt, divided

¼ teaspoon black pepper

2 pounds boneless beef top round or chuck shoulder steak, cut into ½-inch pieces

1 medium onion, chopped, plus additional for garnish

2 cloves garlic, minced

1¼ cups water

¼ cup chili powder

1 teaspoon dried oregano

1 teaspoon ground cumin

½ to 1 teaspoon ground red pepper

½ teaspoon hot pepper sauce

1. Press Sauté; cook bacon in Instant Pot® until crisp. Remove to paper towel-lined plate.

2. Combine flour, ½ teaspoon salt and black pepper in large resealable food storage bag. Add beef; toss to coat. Shake off any excess flour mixture. Add beef to bacon drippings in two batches; cook until browned on all sides. Remove to plate.

3. Add onion to pot; cook and stir 3 minutes or until softened. Add garlic; cook and stir 1 minute. Return beef and bacon to pot. Add water, chili powder, remaining 1 teaspoon salt, oregano, cumin, red pepper and hot pepper sauce; cook and stir 2 minutes, scraping up browned bits from bottom of pot.

4. Secure lid and move pressure release valve to Sealing position. Press Manual; cook at high pressure 20 minutes.

5. When cooking is complete, use natural release for 10 minutes, then release remaining pressure. Serve with additional chopped onion, if desired.

MAKES 4 TO 6 SERVINGS

TIP: Texas chili doesn't contain any beans. But if you want to stretch this recipe and dilute some of the spiciness—and you don't live in Texas!—you can add canned pinto beans to the chili after the pressure has been released. Press Sauté and cook until the beans are heated through.

TUSCAN BEEF STEW

¼ cup dried porcini mushrooms

½ cup hot water

3 slices bacon, chopped

1 tablespoon olive oil

2 pounds beef stew meat, cut into ½-inch pieces

1 teaspoon salt, divided

½ teaspoon black pepper, divided

3 cups assorted mushrooms (portobello, shiitake and/or cremini), sliced

2 cloves garlic, minced

1 teaspoon dried rosemary

1 can (about 14 ounces) diced tomatoes, drained

1 cup frozen pearl onions, thawed

1 cup baby carrots, cut into ½-inch pieces

¼ cup tomato paste

¼ cup dry red wine

2 tablespoons all-purpose flour

Hot cooked pasta (optional)

1. Place dried mushrooms in small bowl; cover with hot water. Let stand about 15 minutes or until softened.

2. Meanwhile, press Sauté; cook bacon in Instant Pot® until crisp. Remove to paper towel-lined plate. Drain off all but 1 tablespoon drippings. Add oil to pot. Season beef with ¼ teaspoon salt and ¼ teaspoon pepper; cook in two batches 6 to 8 minutes or until browned. Remove to plate. Drain mushrooms; strain and reserve soaking liquid. Coarsely chop mushrooms.

3. Add chopped dried mushrooms, soaking liquid, sliced mushrooms, garlic and rosemary to pot; cook and stir 3 minutes, scraping up browned bits from bottom of pot. Stir in beef, tomatoes, onions, carrots, tomato paste, wine, remaining ¾ teaspoon salt and ¼ teaspoon pepper; mix well.

4. Secure lid and move pressure release valve to Sealing position. Press Manual; cook at high pressure 30 minutes.

5. When cooking is complete, use natural release for 10 minutes, then release remaining pressure.

6. Place flour in small bowl; stir in ¼ cup hot liquid from pot until smooth. Press Sauté; add flour mixture to pot. Cook and stir about 3 minutes or until stew thickens. Serve over pasta, if desired.

MAKES 6 TO 8 SERVINGS

SIMPLE SLOPPY JOES

1½ pounds ground
   beef

1 red bell pepper,
   chopped

½ cup chopped onion

1 clove garlic, minced

¼ cup ketchup

¼ cup barbecue
   sauce

2 tablespoons cider
   vinegar

1 tablespoon
   Worcestershire
   sauce

1 tablespoon packed
   brown sugar

1 teaspoon chili
   powder

1 can (about
   8 ounces)
   baked beans

6 sandwich rolls, split

¾ cup (3 ounces)
   shredded Cheddar
   cheese (optional)

1. Press Sauté; add beef to Instant Pot®. Cook about
   8 minutes or until browned, stirring frequently. Drain
   off fat and excess liquid. Add bell pepper, onion and
   garlic to pot; cook and stir 3 minutes. Add ketchup,
   barbecue sauce, vinegar, Worcestershire sauce, brown
   sugar and chili powder; mix well.

2. Secure lid and move pressure release valve to Sealing
   position. Press Manual; cook at high pressure 10 minutes.

3. When cooking is complete, press Cancel and use quick
   release.

4. Press Sauté; add beans to pot. Cook 5 minutes or until
   beef mixture thickens, stirring frequently.

5. Serve beef mixture on rolls; sprinkle with cheese, if
   desired.

MAKES 6 SERVINGS

BEEF POT PIE

⅓ cup all-purpose flour

1½ teaspoons salt, divided

½ teaspoon black pepper, divided

1½ pounds beef stew meat, cut into 1-inch pieces

2 tablespoons olive oil

¾ cup beef broth

½ cup stout, dark beer or ale

1 teaspoon chopped fresh thyme *or* ½ teaspoon dried thyme

1 pound new red potatoes, cut into 1-inch pieces

2 cups baby carrots, halved crosswise

1 cup frozen pearl onions, thawed *or* 1 large onion, chopped

1 parsnip, peeled and cut into 1-inch pieces

1 refrigerated pie crust (half of 15-ounce package)

1. Combine flour, ½ teaspoon salt and ¼ teaspoon pepper in large resealable food storage bag. Add beef; toss to coat. Shake off any excess flour mixture.

2. Press Sauté; heat oil in Instant Pot®. Add beef in two batches; cook until browned on all sides. Stir in broth, stout, thyme, remaining 1 teaspoon salt and ¼ teaspoon pepper; mix well.

3. Secure lid and move pressure release valve to Sealing position. Press Manual; cook at high pressure 25 minutes.

4. When cooking is complete, press Cancel and use quick release. Add potatoes, carrots, onions and parsnip to pot. Secure lid and move pressure release valve to Sealing position. Press Manual; cook at high pressure 15 minutes. Meanwhile, remove pie crust from refrigerator; let stand at room temperature 15 minutes. Preheat oven to 425°F.

5. When cooking is complete, press Cancel and use quick release. Pour beef mixture into 2½- to 3-quart baking dish. Place pie crust over filling; press edges to seal. Cut slits in crust to vent.

6. Bake 15 to 20 minutes or until crust is golden brown. Cool slightly before serving.

MAKES 4 TO 6 SERVINGS

SOUTHWESTERN CHILE BEEF

2 tablespoons vegetable oil

2 pounds beef round roast, cut into bite-size pieces

1 onion, finely chopped

2 cloves garlic, minced

1 teaspoon all-purpose flour

1 teaspoon salt

1 teaspoon dried oregano

½ teaspoon ground cumin

¼ teaspoon black pepper

5 canned whole green chiles, chopped

1 canned chipotle pepper in adobo sauce, chopped

Hot cooked polenta, rice or pasta (optional)

1. Press Sauté; heat 1 tablespoon oil in Instant Pot®. Add half of beef; cook about 5 minutes or until browned, stirring occasionally. Remove to plate. Add remaining oil and beef; cook 3 minutes, stirring occasionally. Add onion and garlic; cook and stir 3 minutes or until beef is browned and onion is softened. Return first half of beef to pot. Add flour, salt, oregano, cumin and black pepper; cook and stir 30 seconds. Stir in green chiles and chipotle pepper; mix well.

2. Secure lid and move pressure release valve to Sealing position. Press Manual; cook at high pressure 35 minutes.

3. When cooking is complete, use natural release for 5 minutes, then release remaining pressure.

4. Press Sauté; cook 5 to 10 minutes or until sauce is reduced and thickens slightly. Serve over polenta, if desired.

MAKES 4 SERVINGS

CLASSIC BEEF STEW

2½ pounds cubed beef stew meat

¼ cup all-purpose flour

1½ teaspoons salt, divided

2 tablespoons olive oil

1 cup beef broth

1 medium onion, chopped

1 ounce dried oyster mushrooms, chopped

2 teaspoons garlic powder

1 teaspoon dried basil

1 teaspoon dried oregano

½ teaspoon dried rosemary

½ teaspoon dried marjoram

½ teaspoon dried sage

½ teaspoon dried thyme

8 fingerling potatoes, halved lengthwise

1 cup baby carrots

Black pepper

Chopped fresh Italian parsley (optional)

1. Combine beef, flour and ½ teaspoon salt in large resealable food storage bag; toss to coat. Shake off any excess flour mixture. Press Sauté; heat oil in Instant Pot®. Add beef in two batches; cook about 5 minutes or until browned. Remove to plate.

2. Add broth, onion, mushrooms, garlic powder, remaining 1 teaspoon salt, basil, oregano, rosemary, marjoram, sage and thyme to pot; mix well. Secure lid and move pressure release valve to Sealing position. Press Manual; cook at high pressure 30 minutes.

3. When cooking is complete, press Cancel and use quick release.

4. Add potatoes and carrots to pot. Secure lid and move pressure release valve to Sealing position. Press Manual; cook at high pressure 10 minutes.

5. When cooking is complete, press Cancel and use quick release. Season with additional salt and pepper, if desired. Garnish with parsley.

MAKES 8 SERVINGS

BARBECUED BEEF SANDWICHES

¾ cup ketchup

2 tablespoons cider vinegar

2 tablespoons dark molasses

1 tablespoon Worcestershire sauce

2 cloves garlic, minced

¾ teaspoon salt

½ teaspoon black pepper

¼ teaspoon dry mustard

¼ teaspoon red pepper flakes

1 medium onion, chopped

1 boneless beef chuck shoulder roast (about 3 pounds), cut into 3 pieces

Sesame seed buns, split

1. Combine ketchup, vinegar, molasses, Worcestershire sauce, garlic, salt, black pepper, mustard and red pepper flakes in medium bowl; mix well. Reserve ⅓ cup mixture; set aside.

2. Spread onion in bottom of Instant Pot®; place beef on top of onion. Pour remaining ketchup mixture over beef.

3. Secure lid and move pressure release valve to Sealing position. Press Manual; cook at high pressure 50 minutes.

4. When cooking is complete, use natural release for 10 minutes, then release remaining pressure. Remove beef to large bowl; let stand until cool enough to handle. Meanwhile, press Sauté; cook liquid in pot until reduced by about half.

5. Shred beef into bite-size pieces, discarding excess fat. Return shredded beef to pot with reserved ketchup mixture; cook and stir until beef is coated and sauce thickens slightly.

6. Spoon beef mixture into sandwich buns.

MAKES 12 SERVINGS

CREOLE-SPICED POT ROAST

2 tablespoons Creole or Cajun seasoning

1 boneless beef chuck roast (3 pounds), cut in half

1 tablespoon vegetable oil

1 medium onion, chopped

1 can (about 14 ounces) diced tomatoes, drained

1 can (about 14 ounces) diced tomatoes with mild green chiles, drained

2 tablespoons hot pepper sauce

1 teaspoon sugar

½ teaspoon black pepper

1 cup chopped rutabaga

1 cup chopped mushrooms

1 cup chopped turnip

1 cup chopped parsnip

1 cup chopped green bell pepper

1 cup green beans

1 cup sliced carrots

1 cup corn

1. Rub Creole seasoning into all sides of beef. Press Sauté; heat oil in Instant Pot®. Add beef; cook about 8 minutes or until browned on all sides. Add onion to pot during last few minutes of browning, stirring until softened. Add tomatoes, hot pepper sauce, sugar and black pepper; mix well.

2. Secure lid and move pressure release valve to Sealing position. Press Manual; cook at high pressure 65 minutes.

3. When cooking is complete, press Cancel and use quick release. Add rutabaga, mushrooms, turnip, parsnip, bell pepper, green beans, carrots and corn to pot, pressing vegetables into liquid.

4. Secure lid and move pressure release valve to Sealing position. Press Manual; cook at high pressure 10 minutes.

5. When cooking is complete, press Cancel and use quick release.

MAKES 6 SERVINGS

1 pound beef stew
   meat, cut into
   1-inch pieces

1 can (about
   15 ounces) pinto
   beans, rinsed
   and drained

1 can (about
   15 ounces) black
   beans, rinsed
   and drained

1 can (about
   14 ounces)
   beef broth

1 can (about
   10 ounces) diced
   tomatoes with
   green chiles

1 green bell pepper,
   cut into ½-inch
   slices

1 red bell pepper, cut
   into ½-inch slices

1 onion, cut into
   ¼-inch slices

2 teaspoons
   ground cumin

1 teaspoon
   seasoned salt

½ teaspoon black
   pepper

Optional toppings:
sour cream,
shredded Monterey
Jack or Cheddar
cheese, chopped
olives

1. Combine beef, beans, broth, tomatoes, bell peppers, onion, cumin, seasoned salt and black pepper in Instant Pot®; mix well.

2. Secure lid and move pressure release valve to Sealing position. Press Manual; cook at high pressure 25 minutes.

3. When cooking is complete, use natural release for 10 minutes, then release remaining pressure. Serve with desired toppings.

MAKES 8 SERVINGS

ONE-POT CHILI MAC

1 pound ground beef
1 cup chopped onion
1 clove garlic, minced
1 tablespoon chili powder
½ teaspoon dried oregano
½ teaspoon ground cumin
¼ teaspoon red pepper flakes
2 cups uncooked macaroni
1 can (about 14 ounces) diced tomatoes
¼ cup water
1 teaspoon salt
¼ teaspoon black pepper

1. Press Sauté; add beef, onion and garlic to Instant Pot®. Cook about 6 minutes or until beef is no longer pink, stirring frequently. Add chili powder, oregano, cumin and red pepper flakes; cook and stir 1 minute. Stir in macaroni, tomatoes, water, salt and black pepper; mix well.

2. Secure lid and move pressure release valve to Sealing position. Press Manual; cook at high pressure 5 minutes.

3. When cooking is complete, press Cancel and use quick release.

MAKES 4 SERVINGS

2½ pounds meaty beef oxtails

1 large onion, cut in half and sliced

4 carrots, cut into ¾-inch pieces, divided

3 stalks celery, cut into ¾-inch pieces, divided

2 sprigs fresh parsley

2 cloves garlic, peeled

½ teaspoon salt

1 bay leaf

5 whole black peppercorns

2 cups beef broth

1 cup dark beer or stout

1 large russet potato, cut into 1-inch pieces

Ground black pepper

Chopped fresh parsley (optional)

1. Combine oxtails, onion, half of carrots, one third of celery, parsley sprigs, garlic, ½ teaspoon salt, bay leaf and peppercorns in Instant Pot®. Stir in broth and beer.

2. Secure lid and move pressure release valve to Sealing position. Press Manual; cook at high pressure 35 minutes.

3. When cooking is complete, use natural release for 5 minutes, then release remaining pressure. Remove oxtails to plate.

4. Strain broth through large sieve or colander, pressing vegetables lightly with slotted spoon to extract all liquid. Discard vegetables. Wipe out pot with paper towels, if necessary. Return broth to pot with remaining half of carrots, two thirds of celery and potato.

5. Secure lid and move pressure release valve to Sealing position. Press Manual; cook at high pressure 3 minutes. When cooking is complete, press Cancel and use quick release.

6. Remove meat from oxtails when cool enough to handle, discarding fat and bones. Press Sauté; add meat to soup. Cook 2 minutes or until heated through. Season with additional salt and pepper; garnish with chopped parsley.

MAKES 4 SERVINGS

TIP: You can use any beer in this recipe, but dark beer—such as bock, stout, or porter—adds extra flavor because the malt in the beer has been roasted before brewing.

SAUCY BBQ SHORT RIBS

¾ cup regular cola (not diet)

1 can (6 ounces) tomato paste

⅓ cup plus 1 tablespoon honey, divided

⅓ cup cider vinegar

2 cloves garlic, minced

1 teaspoon salt

1 teaspoon black pepper

¼ teaspoon hot pepper sauce (optional)

4 pounds bone-in beef short ribs, trimmed and cut into 2-inch pieces

1. Combine cola, tomato paste, ⅓ cup honey, vinegar, garlic, salt, black pepper and hot pepper sauce, if desired, in Instant Pot®; mix well. Add short ribs; turn to coat with sauce.

2. Secure lid and move pressure release valve to Sealing position. Press Manual; cook at high pressure 30 minutes.

3. When cooking is complete, use natural release for 10 minutes, then release remaining pressure. Remove short ribs to plate; tent with foil.

4. Skim excess fat from surface of sauce. Press Sauté; cook 10 to 15 minutes or until sauce is reduced by one third. Add remaining 1 tablespoon honey; cook and stir 1 minute. Brush short ribs with sauce; serve remaining sauce on the side.

MAKES 4 SERVINGS

TIP: For a thicker sauce, whisk 2 tablespoons water into 2 tablespoons cornstarch in a small bowl until smooth. Add to the sauce with the honey in step 4; cook and stir 1 minute or until sauce thickens.

BEEF STEW WITH A COFFEE KICK

⅓ cup all-purpose flour

1 teaspoon salt

1 teaspoon dried marjoram

½ teaspoon garlic powder

½ teaspoon black pepper

2 pounds beef stew meat, cut into 1-inch pieces

2 tablespoons vegetable oil

3 small onions, cut into wedges

¾ cup strong brewed coffee, at room temperature

1 can (about 14 ounces) diced tomatoes

1 bay leaf

2 cups diced peeled potatoes (½-inch pieces)

4 stalks celery, cut into ½-inch slices

4 medium carrots, cut into ½-inch slices

1. Combine flour, salt, marjoram, garlic powder and pepper in large resealable food storage bag. Add beef; toss to coat. Shake off any excess flour mixture.

2. Press Sauté; heat oil in Instant Pot®. Add beef in two batches; cook about 5 minutes or until browned. Remove to plate.

3. Add onions to pot; cook and stir 3 minutes or until softened. Add coffee; cook and stir 1 minute, scraping up browned bits from bottom of pot. Return beef to pot with tomatoes and bay leaf; mix well.

4. Secure lid and move pressure release valve to Sealing position. Press Manual; cook at high pressure 25 minutes.

5. When cooking is complete, use natural release for 5 minutes, then release remaining pressure. Add potatoes, celery and carrots to pot. Secure lid and move pressure release valve to Sealing position. Press Manual; cook at high pressure 12 minutes.

6. When cooking is complete, press Cancel and use quick release. Remove and discard bay leaf. Let stew cool in pot 5 minutes, stirring occasionally. (Stew will thicken as it cools.)

MAKES 6 SERVINGS

MOLE CHILI

2 tablespoons olive oil, divided

1½ pounds boneless beef chuck, cut into 1-inch pieces

2 medium onions, chopped

5 cloves garlic, minced

1 cup beef broth

1 can (about 14 ounces) fire-roasted diced tomatoes

2 corn tortillas, each cut into 4 wedges

2 tablespoons chili powder

1 tablespoon ground ancho chili powder

1 teaspoon dried oregano

1 teaspoon ground cumin

¾ teaspoon salt

¾ teaspoon ground cinnamon

½ teaspoon black pepper

1 can (about 15 ounces) red kidney beans, rinsed and drained

1½ ounces semisweet chocolate, chopped

1. Press Sauté; heat 1 tablespoon oil in Instant Pot®. Add beef in two batches; cook about 5 minutes or until browned. Remove to plate. Add remaining 1 tablespoon oil, onions and garlic to pot; cook and stir about 3 minutes or until softened. Stir in ½ cup broth, scraping up browned bits from bottom of pot. Stir in beef, tomatoes, tortillas, remaining ½ cup broth, chili powders, oregano, cumin, salt, cinnamon and pepper; mix well.

2. Secure lid and move pressure release valve to Sealing position. Press Manual; cook at high pressure 30 minutes.

3. When cooking is complete, use natural release for 15 minutes, then release remaining pressure.

4. Press Sauté; add beans and chocolate to pot. Cook and stir 2 minutes or until chocolate is melted and beans are heated through.

MAKES 4 SERVINGS

2 pounds meaty beef bones

2½ tablespoons tomato paste

1 large onion, top and roots removed, brown outer skin intact, cut into wedges

1 large carrot, cut into large pieces

2 stalks celery, cut into large pieces

8 cups water, divided

4 sprigs fresh parsley

1 bay leaf

½ teaspoon salt

3 whole black peppercorns

1. Preheat oven to 450°F. Spread bones in roasting pan; roast 30 minutes or until browned, turning once. Spread tomato paste over bones; top with onion, carrot and celery. Return pan to oven; roast bones and vegetables 30 minutes. Remove bones and vegetables to Instant Pot®.

2. Skim excess fat from roasting pan and discard. Pour 1 cup water into roasting pan; cook and stir 2 minutes over medium-high heat or until liquid is reduced by half, scraping up browned bits from bottom of pan. Pour into pot. Add remaining 7 cups water, parsley, bay leaf, salt and peppercorns; mix well.

3. Secure lid and move pressure release valve to Sealing position. Press Manual; cook at high pressure 90 minutes.

4. When cooking is complete, use natural release.

5. Strain stock into large bowl through fine-mesh strainer or colander lined with several layers of damp cheesecloth; discard solids. To remove fat, cover and refrigerate stock overnight; fat will rise to the top and can be easily skimmed off the next day. Stock can be refrigerated up to 3 days or frozen up to 3 months.

MAKES ABOUT 7 CUPS

CHILI SPICED PORK LOIN

1 boneless pork loin roast
   (2 to 2½ pounds),
   trimmed
1¼ cups orange juice, divided
1 cup chopped onion
2 cloves garlic, minced
1 tablespoon cider vinegar
1½ teaspoons chili powder
1 teaspoon salt
¼ teaspoon dried thyme
¼ teaspoon ground cumin
¼ teaspoon ground
   cinnamon
⅛ teaspoon ground allspice
⅛ teaspoon ground cloves
2 tablespoons olive oil
   Fruit Chutney (recipe
   follows, optional)

1. Place pork in large resealable food storage bag or glass dish. Combine ½ cup orange juice, onion, garlic, vinegar, chili powder, salt, thyme, cumin, cinnamon, allspice and cloves in small bowl; mix well. Pour marinade over pork; seal bag and turn to coat. Refrigerate 2 to 4 hours or overnight.

2. Remove pork from marinade; reserve marinade. Press Sauté; heat oil in Instant Pot®. Add pork; cook about 6 minutes or until browned on all sides. Stir in remaining ¾ cup orange juice and reserved marinade, scraping up browned bits from bottom of pot.

3. Secure lid and move pressure release valve to Sealing position. Press Manual; cook at high pressure 20 minutes.

4. When cooking is complete, use natural release for 10 minutes, then release remaining pressure. Remove pork to cutting board; tent with foil. Let stand 10 minutes before slicing.

5. Meanwhile, prepare Fruit Chutney, if desired. Or press Sauté and cook until liquid is reduced by one third. Serve with pork.

MAKES 4 SERVINGS

FRUIT CHUTNEY: Add ¼ cup apricot preserves or orange marmalade to cooking liquid after removing pork from pot. Press Sauté; cook 10 minutes, stirring occasionally. Add 1 diced mango, ½ cup diced fresh pineapple, 2 minced green onions and 1 tablespoon minced jalapeño pepper; cook and stir 5 minutes. Serve with pork.

THREE-BEAN CHORIZO CHILI

½ cup dried pinto beans, soaked 8 hours or overnight

½ cup dried kidney beans, soaked 8 hours or overnight

½ cup dried black beans, soaked 8 hours or overnight

2 Mexican chorizo sausages (about 6 ounces *each*), casings removed

1 tablespoon vegetable oil

1 large onion, chopped

1 tablespoon salt

1 tablespoon tomato paste

1 tablespoon minced garlic

1 tablespoon chili powder

1 tablespoon ancho chili powder

1 teaspoon chipotle chili powder

2 teaspoons ground cumin

1 teaspoon ground coriander

1 can (28 ounces) crushed tomatoes

2 cups water

Chopped fresh cilantro (optional)

1. Drain and rinse beans. Press Sauté; add chorizo to Instant Pot®. Cook 3 to 4 minutes, stirring to break up meat. Remove to bowl.

2. Heat oil in pot. Add onion; cook and stir 3 minutes or until softened. Add salt, tomato paste, garlic, chili powders, cumin and coriander; cook and stir 1 minute. Stir in tomatoes, water, beans and chorizo; mix well.

3. Secure lid and move pressure release valve to Sealing position. Press Manual; cook at high pressure 20 minutes.

4. When cooking is complete, use natural release for 10 minutes, then release remaining pressure. Garnish with cilantro.

MAKES 6 TO 8 SERVINGS

HONEY GINGER RIBS

2 pounds pork baby back ribs, trimmed and cut into 2-rib sections

4 green onions, chopped

½ cup hoisin sauce, divided

3 tablespoons dry sherry or rice wine

2 tablespoons honey

2 tablespoons soy sauce

1 tablespoon cider vinegar

1 tablespoon packed brown sugar

2 cloves garlic, minced

1 teaspoon minced fresh ginger

¼ teaspoon Chinese five-spice powder

⅓ cup chicken or beef broth

2 tablespoons cornstarch

Sesame seeds (optional)

1. Place ribs in large resealable food storage bag. Combine green onions, ¼ cup hoisin sauce, sherry, honey, soy sauce, vinegar, brown sugar, garlic, ginger and five-spice powder in medium bowl; mix well. Pour marinade over ribs. Seal bag; turn to coat. Refrigerate 2 to 4 hours or overnight, turning occasionally.

2. Pour broth into Instant Pot®; add ribs and marinade. Secure lid and move pressure release valve to Sealing position. Press Manual; cook at high pressure 25 minutes.

3. When cooking is complete, use natural release for 10 minutes, then release remaining pressure. Remove ribs to plate; tent with foil.

4. Skim excess fat from surface of sauce. Place cornstarch in small bowl; stir in 2 tablespoons sauce until smooth. Press Sauté; add cornstarch mixture to pot, stirring constantly. Cook and stir about 2 minutes or until sauce thickens slightly. Add remaining ¼ cup hoisin sauce; cook and stir until heated through.

5. Brush sauce over ribs before serving. Sprinkle with sesame seeds, if desired.

MAKES 4 SERVINGS

JERK PORK AND SWEET POTATO STEW

2 tablespoons all-purpose flour

1 teaspoon salt

¼ teaspoon black pepper

1¼ pounds boneless pork shoulder, cut into 1-inch pieces

2 tablespoons vegetable oil

4 tablespoons minced green onions, divided

1 small jalapeño pepper, seeded and minced

1 clove garlic, minced

⅛ teaspoon ground allspice

1 cup chicken broth

1 large sweet potato, peeled and cut into ¾-inch pieces

1 cup thawed frozen corn

1 tablespoon lime juice

Hot cooked rice (optional)

1. Combine flour, salt and black pepper in large resealable food storage bag. Add pork; toss to coat. Shake off any excess flour. Press Sauté; heat oil in Instant Pot®. Add pork in two batches, cook about 5 minutes or until browned. Remove to plate.

2. Add 2 tablespoons green onions, jalapeño, garlic and allspice to pot; cook and stir 30 seconds. Stir in broth, scraping up browned bits from bottom of pot. Return pork to pot.

3. Secure lid and move pressure release valve to Sealing position. Press Manual; cook at high pressure 18 minutes. When cooking is complete, press Cancel and use quick release.

4. Add sweet potato to pot. Secure lid and move pressure release valve to Sealing position. Press Manual; cook at high pressure 2 minutes.

5. When cooking is complete, press Cancel and use quick release.

6. Stir in corn, remaining 2 tablespoons green onions and lime juice; let stand 2 minutes or until corn is heated through. Serve with rice, if desired.

MAKES 4 SERVINGS

BEER BARBECUED PULLED PORK SANDWICHES

1 tablespoon chili powder

½ teaspoon salt

¼ teaspoon black pepper

2 pounds boneless pork shoulder, trimmed and cut into 3-inch pieces

1 tablespoon vegetable oil

1 cup chopped onion

½ cup ale or dark beer*

⅓ cup ketchup

¼ cup chicken broth

3 tablespoons honey

2 tablespoons cider vinegar

2 tablespoons whole grain mustard

8 sandwich rolls, split

Bread-and-butter pickle chips

*For best flavor, do not use light beer.

1. Combine chili powder, salt and pepper in small bowl; mix well. Rub mixture into all sides of pork.

2. Press Sauté; heat oil in Instant Pot®. Add pork in batches; cook about 8 minutes or until browned. Remove to plate. Add onion, beer, ketchup, broth, honey, vinegar and mustard to pot; cook and stir 2 minutes, scraping up browned bits from bottom of pot. Return pork to pot, pressing into liquid.

3. Secure lid and move pressure release valve to Sealing position. Press Manual; cook at high pressure 45 minutes.

4. When cooking is complete, use natural release for 10 minutes, then release remaining pressure. Remove pork to clean plate.

5. Skim excess fat from surface of sauce. Press Sauté; cook about 10 minutes or until sauce is reduced by one third. Meanwhile, shred pork into bite-size pieces when cool enough to handle.

6. Combine pork and 1 cup sauce in large bowl; toss to coat. Add additional sauce if necessary. Serve on rolls with pickles.

MAKES 8 SERVINGS

PORK ROAST WITH TART CHERRIES

3 teaspoons grated horseradish, divided

2 teaspoons ground coriander

¾ teaspoon salt

½ teaspoon black pepper

1 tablespoon olive oil

1 boneless pork loin roast (about 2 pounds), trimmed

1 can (about 14 ounces) pitted tart cherries, undrained

¼ cup dry sherry, Madeira or white wine

4 teaspoons grated orange peel

1 tablespoon packed brown sugar

1 tablespoon Dijon mustard

⅛ teaspoon ground cloves

Orange slices (optional)

Fresh Italian parsley sprigs (optional)

1. Combine 2 teaspoons horseradish, coriander, salt and pepper in small bowl; mix well. Press Sauté; heat oil in Instant Pot®. Add pork; cook about 10 minutes or until browned on all sides. Remove to plate; rub horseradish mixture evenly over all sides of pork.

2. Drain cherries, reserving ¼ cup liquid. Add cherries, reserved cherry liquid and sherry to pot; cook about 4 minutes or until half of liquid is evaporated, scraping up browned bits from bottom of pot. Place rack in pot; place pork on rack.

3. Secure lid and move pressure release valve to Sealing position. Press Manual; cook at high pressure 25 minutes.

4. When cooking is complete, use natural release for 10 minutes, then release remaining pressure. Remove pork to plate; tent with foil.

5. Strain cooking liquid into medium bowl, reserving cherries. Return liquid to pot. Press Sauté; stir in orange peel, brown sugar, mustard, remaining 1 teaspoon horseradish and cloves. Cook 10 minutes or until sauce thickens slightly, stirring occasionally. Stir in reserved cherries. Serve sauce with pork; garnish with orange slices and parsley.

MAKES 4 SERVINGS

TIP: If you like spicier food, double the amount of the horseradish, coriander, and pepper used for the rub.

CHILI VERDE

1 tablespoon vegetable oil

1 pound boneless pork loin, cut into 1-inch pieces

1 onion, halved and thinly sliced

1 pound tomatillos, husks removed, rinsed and coarsely chopped

6 cloves garlic, minced

1 teaspoon ground cumin

1 can (about 15 ounces) Great Northern beans, rinsed and drained

1 can (4 ounces) diced green chiles

1 teaspoon salt

¼ teaspoon black pepper

¼ cup chopped fresh cilantro

1. Press Sauté; heat oil in Instant Pot®. Add pork; cook about 6 minutes or until browned. Remove to plate.

2. Add onion to pot; cook and stir 3 minutes or until softened. Add tomatillos, garlic and cumin; cook and stir 3 minutes, scraping up browned bits from bottom of pot. Stir in beans, chiles, salt, pepper and pork; mix well.

3. Secure lid and move pressure release valve to Sealing position. Press Manual; cook at high pressure 8 minutes.

4. When cooking is complete, use natural release for 10 minutes, then release remaining pressure. Stir in cilantro.

MAKES 4 SERVINGS

CHIPOTLE PORK TACOS

1 tablespoon vegetable oil

1 cup chopped onion

4 cloves garlic, minced

½ teaspoon ground cumin

1 can (8 ounces) tomato sauce

¼ cup water

3 tablespoons cider vinegar, divided

2 chipotle peppers in adobo sauce, finely chopped

1 teaspoon salt

2½ pounds boneless pork shoulder, trimmed and cut into 3-inch pieces

Roasted Green Onions (recipe follows, optional)

16 (6-inch) corn tortillas

1. Press Sauté; heat oil in Instant Pot®. Add onion; cook and stir 3 minutes or until softened. Add garlic and cumin; cook and stir 30 seconds. Stir in tomato sauce, water, 2 tablespoons vinegar, chipotle peppers and salt; mix well. Add pork to pot, pressing into liquid.

2. Secure lid and move pressure release valve to Sealing position. Press Manual; cook at high pressure 45 minutes.

3. When cooking is complete, use natural release for 10 minutes, then release remaining pressure. Remove pork to plate.

4. Skim excess fat from surface of sauce. Stir in remaining 1 tablespoon vinegar. Press Sauté; cook about 15 minutes or until sauce is reduced by half and thickens slightly, stirring occasionally.

5. Meanwhile, prepare Roasted Green Onions, if desired. Shred pork into bite-sized pieces. Combine pork and 1 cup sauce in large bowl; toss to coat. Add additional sauce if necessary.

6. Heat tortillas over stovetop burner or grill about 15 seconds per side or until lightly charred. Fill tortillas with pork mixture and Roasted Green Onions.

MAKES 6 TO 8 SERVINGS

ROASTED GREEN ONIONS: Preheat oven to 425°F. Trim 16 green onions; place on large baking sheet. Drizzle with 1 tablespoon olive oil; toss gently to coat. Arrange in single layer; roast 10 minutes. Sprinkle with salt.

HOT AND SWEET SAUSAGE SANDWICHES

1½ cups pasta sauce

1 large sweet onion, cut into ¼-inch slices

1 medium green bell pepper, cut into ½-inch slices

1 medium red bell pepper, cut into ½-inch slices

1½ tablespoons packed dark brown sugar

1 package (16 ounces) hot Italian sausage links (5 sausages)

5 Italian rolls, split

1. Combine pasta sauce, onion, bell peppers and brown sugar in Instant Pot®; mix well. Add sausages to pot; spoon some of sauce mixture over sausages.

2. Secure lid and move pressure release valve to Sealing position. Press Manual; cook at high pressure 5 minutes.

3. When cooking is complete, use natural release for 10 minutes, then release remaining pressure. Remove sausages to plate; tent with foil.

4. Press Sauté; cook 10 minutes or until sauce is reduced by one third, stirring occasionally. Serve sausages in rolls; top with sauce.

MAKES 5 SERVINGS

TIP: Refrigerate or freeze leftover sauce; serve over pasta or polenta. Top with grated Parmesan cheese.

1 cup chicken broth

¼ cup dry sherry

3 tablespoons soy sauce

1 tablespoon hoisin sauce

1½ tablespoons cornstarch

2 tablespoons vegetable oil

1½ pounds boneless pork shoulder, trimmed and cut into 1-inch pieces

1 large onion, chopped

3 cloves garlic, minced

1 teaspoon Chinese five-spice powder

½ teaspoon salt

2 cups baby carrots

1 large green bell pepper, cut into 1-inch pieces

1. Combine broth, sherry, soy sauce and hoisin sauce in medium bowl; mix well. Stir 3 tablespoons broth mixture into cornstarch in small bowl until smooth; set aside to thicken stew after cooking.

2. Press Sauté; heat oil in Instant Pot®. Add pork in two batches; cook about 5 minutes or until browned. Remove to plate.

3. Add onion to pot; cook and stir 3 minutes or until softened. Add garlic, five-spice powder and salt; cook and stir 30 seconds. Add broth mixture; cook and stir 1 minute, scraping up browned bits from bottom of pot. Return pork to pot.

4. Secure lid and move pressure release valve to Sealing position. Press Manual; cook at high pressure 15 minutes.

5. When cooking is complete, press Cancel and use quick release. Add carrots and bell pepper to pot. Secure lid and move pressure release valve to Sealing position. Press Manual; cook at high pressure 2 minutes. When cooking is complete, press Cancel and use quick release.

6. Stir reserved cornstarch mixture. Press Sauté; add cornstarch mixture to pot, stirring constantly. Cook and stir about 1 minute or until stew thickens.

MAKES 6 SERVINGS

PORK LOIN WITH APPLES AND ONIONS

2 tablespoons vegetable oil

1 bone-in or boneless pork loin roast (about 3 pounds), trimmed

2 medium onions, chopped

2 sweet-tart apples such as Braeburn, Honeycrisp or Jonagold, peeled and thinly sliced

1 cup lager beer

2 tablespoons packed brown sugar

1 teaspoon ground ginger

½ teaspoon salt

½ teaspoon ground cinnamon

½ teaspoon black pepper

⅛ teaspoon ground red pepper

1. Press Sauté; heat oil in Instant Pot®. Add pork; cook about 8 minutes or until browned on all sides. Remove to plate.

2. Add onions to pot; cook and stir 5 minutes or until lightly browned. Add apples, beer, brown sugar, ginger, salt, cinnamon, black pepper and red pepper; cook and stir 1 minute, scraping up browned bits from bottom of pot. Return pork to pot.

3. Secure lid and move pressure release valve to Sealing position. Press Manual; cook at high pressure 35 minutes.

4. When cooking is complete, use natural release for 10 minutes, then release remaining pressure. Remove pork to cutting board; tent with foil.

5. Press Sauté; cook about 10 minutes or until sauce is reduced by one third, stirring occasionally. Serve with pork.

MAKES 4 SERVINGS

2 cups water

2 tablespoons salt

1 tablespoon sugar

1 teaspoon dried
   thyme

1 bay leaf

½ teaspoon black
   pepper

1 boneless pork
   loin roast (3 to
   3½ pounds)

1 tablespoon olive oil

⅓ cup dry red wine

   Juice of ½ lemon

2 cloves garlic,
   minced

2 cups green grapes

1 cup dried apricots

1 cup dried prunes

1. Combine water, salt, sugar, thyme, bay leaf and pepper in large resealable food storage bag. Add pork; seal bag and refrigerate overnight or up to 2 days, turning occasionally.

2. Remove pork from brine; discard liquid. Pat dry with paper towels. Press Sauté; heat oil in Instant Pot®. Add pork; cook about 10 minutes or until browned on all sides. Remove to plate. Add wine, lemon juice and garlic; cook and stir 1 minute, scraping up browned bits from bottom of pot. Stir in grapes, apricots and prunes; mix well. Return pork to pot.

3. Secure lid and move pressure release valve to Sealing position. Press Manual; cook at high pressure 20 minutes.

4. When cooking is complete, use natural release. Remove pork to cutting board; tent with foil and let stand 10 minutes.

5. Meanwhile, press Sauté; cook 10 minutes or until sauce is reduced and thickens slightly. Slice pork; serve with sauce.

MAKES 8 SERVINGS

CIDER PORK AND ONIONS

1 tablespoon vegetable oil

1 bone-in pork shoulder roast (4 to 4½ pounds)*

4 onions, cut into ¼-inch slices (about 4 cups)

1 cup apple cider, divided

1 teaspoon salt, divided

4 cloves garlic, minced

1 teaspoon dried rosemary

½ teaspoon black pepper

*A 4-pound roast requires a pressure cooker that is 8 quarts or larger to fit.

1. Press Sauté; heat oil in Instant Pot®. Add pork; cook until browned on all sides. Remove to plate. Add onions, ¼ cup cider and ½ teaspoon salt to pot; cook 8 minutes or until onions are softened, scraping up browned bits from bottom of pot. Add garlic and rosemary, cook and stir 1 minute. Return pork to pot; sprinkle with remaining ½ teaspoon salt and pepper. Pour remaining ¾ cup cider over pork.

2. Secure lid and move pressure release valve to Sealing position. Cook at high pressure 75 minutes.

3. When cooking is complete, use natural release. Remove pork to large platter; tent with foil.

4. Meanwhile, press Sauté; cook 10 to 15 minutes or until sauce is reduced by one third. Skim fat from sauce; season with additional salt and pepper, if desired. Cut pork; serve with sauce.

MAKES 8 SERVINGS

PORK PICADILLO

1 tablespoon olive oil

1 pound boneless pork country-style ribs, trimmed and cut into ½-inch pieces

1 onion, chopped

2 cloves garlic, minced

1 can (about 14 ounces) diced tomatoes

½ cup raisins

2 tablespoons cider vinegar

2 canned chipotle peppers in adobo sauce, chopped

½ teaspoon salt

½ teaspoon ground cumin

½ teaspoon ground cinnamon

1. Press Sauté; heat oil in Instant Pot®. Add pork; cook and stir about 6 minutes or until browned. Add onion; cook and stir 2 minutes. Add garlic; cook and stir 30 seconds. Stir in tomatoes, raisins, vinegar, chipotle peppers, salt, cumin and cinnamon, scraping up browned bits from bottom of pot.

2. Secure lid and move pressure release valve to Sealing position. Press Manual; cook at high pressure 25 minutes.

3. When cooking is complete, use natural release for 10 minutes, then release remaining pressure. Stir pork mixture with tongs, shredding pork into smaller pieces.

MAKES 4 SERVINGS

CHORIZO BURRITOS

15 ounces Mexican chorizo sausages, casings removed, cut into bite-size pieces

2 green or red bell peppers, cut into 1-inch pieces

1 can (about 15 ounces) red beans, rinsed and drained

1 can (about 14 ounces) diced tomatoes

1 can (11 ounces) corn, drained

½ teaspoon ground cumin

½ teaspoon ground cinnamon

8 (8-inch) flour tortillas, warmed

2 cups hot cooked rice

½ cup (2 ounces) shredded Monterey Jack cheese

1. Combine chorizo, bell peppers, beans, tomatoes, corn, cumin and cinnamon in Instant Pot®; mix well.

2. Secure lid and move pressure release valve to Sealing position. Press Manual; cook at high pressure 10 minutes.

3. When cooking is complete, use natural release for 10 minutes, then release remaining pressure.

4. Press Sauté; cook about 5 minutes or until chorizo mixture thickens, stirring occasionally. Spoon mixture down centers of tortillas; top with rice and shredded cheese. Roll up tortillas; serve immediately.

MAKES 4 SERVINGS

ALE'D PORK AND SAUERKRAUT

2 teaspoons paprika

1 teaspoon garlic powder

½ teaspoon salt

¼ teaspoon black pepper

1 boneless pork shoulder or pork butt roast (about 3½ pounds), trimmed

1½ tablespoons vegetable oil

1 jar (32 ounces) sauerkraut, drained

1 bottle or can (12 ounces) ale or dark beer

1 tablespoon sugar

1. Combine paprika, garlic powder, salt and pepper in small bowl; mix well. Rub mixture into all sides of pork.

2. Press Sauté; heat oil in Instant Pot®. Add pork; cook 8 minutes or until browned on all sides. Remove to plate.

3. Add sauerkraut, ale and sugar to pot; cook and stir 2 minutes, scraping up browned bits from bottom of pot. Return pork to pot, pressing into sauerkraut mixture.

4. Secure lid and move pressure release valve to Sealing position. Press Manual; cook at high pressure 45 minutes.

5. When cooking is complete, use natural release for 10 minutes, then release remaining pressure. Remove pork to cutting board; tent with foil. Let stand 10 minutes before slicing. Serve with sauerkraut and cooking liquid remaining in pot.

MAKES 4 TO 6 SERVINGS

MAPLE SPICE RUBBED RIBS

3 teaspoons chili powder, divided

1¼ teaspoons ground coriander

1¼ teaspoons garlic powder, divided

¾ teaspoon salt

½ teaspoon black pepper

3 to 3½ pounds pork baby back ribs, trimmed and cut into 4-rib sections

4 tablespoons maple syrup, divided

1 can (8 ounces) tomato sauce

¼ teaspoon ground cinnamon

¼ teaspoon ground ginger

1. Combine 1½ teaspoons chili powder, coriander, ¾ teaspoon garlic powder, salt and pepper in small bowl; mix well. Brush ribs with 2 tablespoons maple syrup; rub with spice mixture. Place ribs in Instant Pot®.

2. Combine tomato sauce, remaining 2 tablespoons maple syrup, 1½ teaspoons chili powder, ½ teaspoon garlic powder, cinnamon and ginger in medium bowl; mix well. Pour over ribs in pot; stir to coat ribs with sauce.

3. Secure lid and move pressure release valve to Sealing position. Press Manual; cook at high pressure 25 minutes.

4. When cooking is complete, use natural release for 10 minutes, then release remaining pressure. Remove ribs to plate; tent with foil.

5. Press Sauté; cook about 10 minutes or until sauce thickens. Brush ribs with sauce; serve remaining sauce on the side.

MAKES 4 SERVINGS

3 cloves garlic, minced

1 teaspoon Greek seasoning

1 teaspoon salt

1 teaspoon black pepper

4 bone-in lamb shoulder chops (¾ to 1 inch thick, about 2 pounds)

3 tablespoons olive oil

1 large onion, sliced

½ cup dry white wine

3 plum tomatoes, each cut into 6 wedges

½ cup pitted kalamata olives

½ cup chicken broth

Chopped fresh parsley

1. Combine garlic, Greek seasoning, salt and pepper in small bowl; mix well. Rub spice mixture into both sides of lamb chops.

2. Press Sauté; heat oil in Instant Pot®. Add lamb chops in two batches; cook about 8 minutes or until browned on both sides. Remove to plate. Add onion and wine to pot; cook and stir 3 minutes or until onion is softened and wine is almost evaporated, scraping up browned bits from bottom of pot. Stir in tomatoes, olives and broth; mix well. Return lamb to pot, pressing into tomato mixture.

3. Secure lid and move pressure release valve to Sealing position. Press Manual; cook at high pressure 12 minutes.

4. When cooking is complete, use natural release for 10 minutes, then release remaining pressure. Remove lamb and tomatoes to clean plate; tent with foil.

5. Press Sauté; cook 10 to 15 minutes or sauce is until reduced by one third. Serve sauce over lamb and vegetables; sprinkle with parsley.

MAKES 4 SERVINGS

TIP: To make your own Greek seasoning, combine 1½ teaspoons dried oregano, 1 teaspoon dried mint, 1 teaspoon dried thyme, ½ teaspoon dried basil, ½ teaspoon dried marjoram, ¼ teaspoon onion powder, and ¼ teaspoon garlic powder in a small bowl; mix well. Store in an airtight container.

SPICY-SWEET LAMB TAGINE

¾ cup dried chickpeas, soaked 8 hours or overnight

1 tablespoon olive oil

2 pounds boneless lamb shoulder or leg, cut into 1½-inch pieces

3 medium onions, each cut into 8 wedges

3 cloves garlic, minced

2 teaspoons ground ginger

2 teaspoons ground cinnamon

1 teaspoon black pepper

1½ cups water

1 can (about 14 ounces) diced tomatoes

2 teaspoons salt

1 small butternut squash, peeled and cut into 1-inch pieces (about 3 cups)

1 cup chopped pitted prunes

2 medium zucchini, halved lengthwise and cut crosswise into ½-inch slices

Saffron Couscous (recipe follows, optional)

¼ cup chopped fresh cilantro or parsley

1. Drain and rinse chickpeas. Press Sauté; heat oil in Instant Pot®. Add lamb in two batches; cook about 5 minutes or until browned. Remove to plate.

2. Add onions, garlic, ginger, cinnamon and pepper to pot; cook and stir 30 seconds or until spices are fragrant. Add water; cook and stir 2 minutes, scraping up browned bits from bottom of pot. Stir in tomatoes, chickpeas and salt; mix well. Return lamb to pot.

3. Secure lid and move pressure release valve to Sealing position. Press Manual; cook at high pressure 15 minutes. When cooking is complete, press Cancel and use quick release.

4. Add butternut squash and prunes to pot. Secure lid and move pressure release valve to Sealing position. Press Manual; cook at high pressure 3 minutes. When cooking is complete, press Cancel and use quick release.

5. Press Sauté; add zucchini to pot. Cook 4 minutes or until zucchini is crisp-tender, stirring occasionally.

6. Meanwhile, prepare Saffron Couscous, if desired. Serve stew over couscous. Garnish with cilantro.

MAKES 4 TO 6 SERVINGS

SAFFRON COUSCOUS: Combine 2¼ cups water, 1 tablespoon butter, ¼ teaspoon salt and ¼ teaspoon crushed saffron threads in medium saucepan; bring to a boil over high heat. Stir in 1½ cups uncooked couscous. Remove from heat; cover and let stand 5 minutes or until liquid is absorbed. Fluff with fork.

ITALIAN TOMATO-BRAISED LAMB

1 can (28 ounces) whole plum tomatoes, undrained

4 bone-in lamb shoulder chops (¾ to 1 inch thick, about 2 pounds)

1½ teaspoons dried oregano

½ teaspoon salt

¼ teaspoon black pepper

2 tablespoons olive oil

2 onions, cut into quarters and thinly sliced

3 cloves garlic, minced

2 tablespoons red wine vinegar

3 to 4 sprigs fresh rosemary

Hot cooked polenta or pasta (optional)

1. Drain tomatoes, reserving 1 cup juice. Coarsely chop tomatoes. (Tomatoes can also be broken up with hands or cut with scissors in can.)

2. Season both sides of lamb with oregano, salt and pepper. Press Sauté; heat oil in Instant Pot®. Add onions and garlic; cook and stir 3 minutes or until softened. Add tomatoes, reserved 1 cup juice and vinegar; cook and stir 1 minute. Add lamb and rosemary to pot, pressing into liquid.

3. Secure lid and move pressure release valve to Sealing position. Press Manual; cook at high pressure 12 minutes.

4. When cooking is complete, use natural release for 10 minutes, then release remaining pressure. Remove lamb to plate; cover loosely to keep warm. Remove and discard rosemary sprigs.

5. Press Sauté; cook 5 to 10 minutes or until sauce is reduced by one third. Serve sauce with lamb and polenta, if desired.

MAKES 4 SERVINGS

LAMB AND CHICKPEA STEW

1 cup dried chickpeas, soaked 8 hours or overnight

2 tablespoons vegetable oil, divided

1 pound lamb stew meat

1 large onion, chopped

1 tablespoon minced garlic

1½ teaspoons salt

1½ teaspoons ground cumin

1 teaspoon ground turmeric

1 teaspoon ground coriander

1 teaspoon ground cinnamon

¼ teaspoon black pepper

1½ cups chicken broth

1 can (about 14 ounces) diced tomatoes

½ cup chopped dried apricots, divided

¼ cup chopped fresh Italian parsley

2 tablespoons lemon juice

1 tablespoon honey

Hot cooked couscous

1. Drain and rinse chickpeas. Press Sauté; heat 1 tablespoon oil in Instant Pot®. Add lamb; cook about 6 minutes or until browned. Add remaining 1 tablespoon oil and onion to pot; cook and stir 3 minutes or until softened. Add garlic, salt, cumin, turmeric, coriander, cinnamon and pepper; cook and stir 1 minute. Add broth and tomatoes; cook and stir 2 minutes, scraping up browned bits from bottom of pot. Stir in chickpeas and half of apricots; mix well.

2. Secure lid and move pressure release valve to Sealing position. Press Manual; cook at high pressure 20 minutes.

3. When cooking is complete, use natural release for 10 minutes, then release remaining pressure.

4. Press Sauté; add remaining half of apricots to pot. Cook 5 minutes or until sauce is reduced and thickens slightly, stirring frequently. Stir in parsley, lemon juice and honey. Serve over couscous.

MAKES 4 TO 6 SERVINGS

Italian Country-Style Chicken
(page 72)

Mu Shu Turkey
(page 85)

Chicken Tortilla Soup
(page 60)

POULTRY & SEAFOOD

Sea Bass with Vegetables *(page 88)*

**Basque Chicken
with Peppers**
(page 62)

**Turkey Meatballs with
Cranberry Barbecue Sauce**
(page 84)

**Scallops with Herb
Tomato Sauce**
(page 97)

POULTRY & SEAFOOD

MOROCCAN CHICKEN STEW

2 tablespoons olive oil, divided

1 pound boneless skinless chicken thighs, cut into 2-inch pieces

½ cup chopped onion

½ cup chopped celery

½ cup chopped carrots

3 cloves garlic, minced

½ teaspoon salt

½ teaspoon ground coriander

½ teaspoon ground cinnamon

¼ teaspoon dried oregano

⅛ teaspoon ground ginger

⅛ teaspoon black pepper

¾ cup dry white wine

⅓ cup chopped prunes

2 tablespoons white balsamic vinegar

1 tablespoon packed brown sugar

1 bay leaf

Hot cooked couscous or rice (optional)

1. Press Sauté; heat oil in Instant Pot®. Add chicken; cook and stir about 5 minutes or until no longer pink. Remove to plate. Add remaining 1 tablespoon oil, onion, celery and carrots; cook and stir 3 minutes or until vegetables are softened. Add garlic, salt, coriander, cinnamon, oregano, ginger and pepper; cook and stir 1 minute. Stir in wine, scraping up browned bits from bottom of pot. Stir in prunes, vinegar, brown sugar and bay leaf; mix well.

2. Secure lid and move pressure release valve to Sealing position. Press Manual; cook at high pressure 6 minutes.

3. When cooking is complete, use natural release for 10 minutes, then release remaining pressure. Serve with couscous, if desired.

MAKES 2 TO 3 SERVINGS

CHICKEN CACCIATORE

¼ cup all-purpose flour

½ teaspoon salt

¼ teaspoon black pepper

3 pounds boneless skinless chicken breasts

1 tablespoon olive oil

1 medium onion, sliced

½ cup water

2 teaspoons garlic powder

1 teaspoon dried oregano

1 teaspoon paprika

1 teaspoon ground cumin

⅛ teaspoon ground red pepper

½ medium red bell pepper, sliced

½ medium green bell pepper, sliced

½ medium yellow bell pepper, sliced

1¼ cups grape tomatoes (about 15)

Hot cooked noodles or rice (optional)

1. Combine flour, salt and black pepper in shallow bowl; mix well. Coat chicken with flour mixture; shake off excess.

2. Press Sauté; heat oil in Instant Pot®. Add chicken in two batches; cook about 4 minutes per side or until browned. Remove to plate. Add onion to pot; cook and stir 3 minutes or until softened. Add water, garlic powder, oregano, paprika, cumin and ground red pepper; cook 1 minute, scraping up browned bits from bottom of pot. Add bell peppers and tomatoes; mix well. Return chicken to pot, pressing into vegetable mixture.

3. Secure lid and move pressure release valve to Sealing position. Press Manual; cook at high pressure 10 minutes.

4. When cooking is complete, press Cancel and use quick release.

5. Press Sauté; cook 2 minutes or until sauce thickens slightly. Serve with noodles, if desired.

MAKES 6 SERVINGS

LEMON ROSEMARY CHICKEN AND POTATOES

4 bone-in skinless chicken breasts (about 8 ounces each)

2 pounds small red potatoes, cut into halves or quarters (1½-inch pieces)

1 large onion, cut into 2-inch pieces

½ cup lemon juice

6 tablespoons olive oil

6 cloves garlic, minced

2 tablespoons plus 1 teaspoon finely chopped fresh rosemary leaves *or* 2¼ teaspoons dried rosemary

2 teaspoons grated lemon peel

1½ teaspoons salt

½ teaspoon black pepper

1 tablespoon vegetable oil

½ cup chicken broth

1. Place chicken in large resealable food storage bag. Place potatoes and onion in another resealable bag. Combine lemon juice, olive oil, garlic, rosemary, lemon peel, 1½ teaspoons salt and pepper in small bowl; mix well. Pour half of marinade (about 6 tablespoons) over chicken; pour remaining marinade over potatoes and onion. Seal bags and turn to coat. Refrigerate 2 hours or overnight.

2. Remove chicken from marinade; discard marinade. Press Sauté; heat vegetable oil in Instant Pot®. Add chicken in two batches; cook about 8 minutes or until browned on both sides. Remove to plate.

3. Remove potatoes and onion from marinade; reserve marinade. Add vegetables to pot; cook and stir 3 minutes, scraping up browned bits from bottom of pot. Arrange chicken on top of vegetables; pour reserved marinade and broth over chicken.

4. Secure lid and move pressure release valve to Sealing position. Select Manual; cook at high pressure 9 minutes.

5. When cooking is complete, press Cancel and use quick release. Remove chicken and vegetables to platter; cover loosely to keep warm.

6. Skim excess fat from surface of cooking liquid. Press Sauté; cook about 5 minutes or until sauce is slightly reduced. Season vegetables with additional salt, if desired. Serve sauce over chicken and vegetables.

MAKES 4 SERVINGS

CHICKEN TORTILLA SOUP

2 cans (about 14 ounces each) diced tomatoes

1½ pounds boneless skinless chicken thighs

1 onion, chopped

1 can (4 ounces) diced green chiles

½ cup chicken broth

2 cloves garlic, minced

1 teaspoon ground cumin

1 teaspoon salt

¼ teaspoon black pepper

4 corn tortillas, cut into ¼-inch strips

2 tablespoons chopped fresh cilantro

½ cup (2 ounces) shredded Monterey Jack cheese

1 avocado, diced and tossed with lime juice

Lime wedges

1. Combine tomatoes, chicken, onion, chiles, broth, garlic, cumin, salt and pepper in Instant Pot®; mix well.

2. Secure lid and move pressure release valve to Sealing position. Press Manual; cook at high pressure 9 minutes.

3. When cooking is complete, use natural release for 10 minutes, then release remaining pressure.

4. Remove chicken to plate; shred into bite-size pieces when cool enough to handle. Stir into soup.

5. Press Sauté; add tortillas and cilantro to soup. Cook and stir 2 minutes or until heated through. Top with cheese, avocado and squeeze of lime juice. Serve immediately.*

If desired, soup can be made ahead through step 3. When ready to serve, heat soup to a simmer; add tortilla strips and cilantro and cook until heated through.

MAKES 4 TO 6 SERVINGS

Polenta (recipe follows, optional)

6 plum tomatoes, coarsely chopped

½ teaspoon salt, divided

½ teaspoon garlic powder

½ teaspoon Italian seasoning

¾ teaspoon black pepper, divided

6 boneless skinless chicken breasts (about 8 ounces each)

1 tablespoon vegetable oil

½ cup chopped onion

2 cloves garlic, minced

1 can (8 ounces) tomato sauce

2 teaspoons dried basil

2 teaspoons dried oregano

2 teaspoons dried rosemary

1. Prepare and refrigerate Polenta up to a day in advance, if desired.

2. Place tomatoes in colander; toss with ¼ teaspoon salt. Let tomatoes drain while preparing chicken. Combine garlic powder, Italian seasoning, remaining ¼ teaspoon salt and ¼ teaspoon pepper in small bowl; mix well. Rub spice mixture into both sides of chicken.

3. Press Sauté; heat oil in Instant Pot®. Add chicken in two batches; cook about 8 minutes until browned on both sides. Remove chicken to plate.

4. Add onion to pot; cook and stir 3 minutes or until beginning to brown. Add garlic; cook and stir 15 seconds. Stir in drained plum tomatoes, tomato sauce, basil, oregano, rosemary and remaining ½ teaspoon pepper, scraping up browned bits from bottom of pot. Return chicken to pot, pressing into tomato mixture.

5. Secure lid and move pressure release valve to Sealing position. Press Manual; cook at high pressure 6 minutes.

6. When cooking is complete, press Cancel and use quick release. Remove chicken to clean plate; tent with foil. Press Sauté; cook sauce about 10 minutes or until slightly thickened, stirring occasionally. Serve sauce with chicken and polenta, if desired.

MAKES 6 SERVINGS

POLENTA: Bring 4 cups chicken broth to a boil in large saucepan over high heat. Slowly stir in 1 cup polenta (not instant) or yellow cornmeal. Reduce heat to low; cook 15 to 20 minutes or until very thick, stirring frequently. (Mixture may be lumpy.) Pour polenta into greased 9×5-inch loaf pan. Cool to room temperature; cover and refrigerate 2 to 3 hours or until firm. To serve, remove from pan and cut crosswise into 16 slices. Cut slices into triangles, if desired. Spray large nonstick skillet with nonstick cooking spray; cook polenta over medium heat about 4 minutes per side or until lightly browned.

BASQUE CHICKEN WITH PEPPERS

1 cut-up whole chicken
   (3½ to 4 pounds)*

2 teaspoons salt, divided

1 teaspoon black pepper,
   divided

1½ tablespoons olive oil

1 onion, chopped

2 red, yellow or green
   bell peppers (or a
   combination), cut
   into strips

8 ounces small brown
   mushrooms, halved

2 cloves garlic, minced

1 teaspoon smoked paprika

½ teaspoon dried thyme

1 can (about 14 ounces)
   stewed tomatoes

2 tablespoons tomato paste

1 tablespoon all-purpose
   flour (optional)

2 tablespoons water
   (optional)

4 ounces chopped
   prosciutto

*Or purchase 2 leg quarters
and 2 breasts and cut each
into two pieces.*

1. Season chicken with 1 teaspoon salt and ½ teaspoon black pepper. Press Sauté; heat oil in Instant Pot®. Add chicken in two batches; cook about 8 minutes or until browned on all sides. Remove to plate.

2. Add onion to pot; cook and stir 3 minutes or until softened. Add bell peppers and mushrooms; cook and stir 4 minutes or until mushrooms have released their liquid. Add garlic, smoked paprika and thyme; cook and stir 1 minute. Stir in tomatoes, tomato paste, remaining 1 teaspoon salt and ½ teaspoon black pepper; mix well. Return chicken to pot, arranging legs and thighs on bottom and breasts on top. Spoon some of tomato mixture over chicken.

3. Secure lid and move pressure release valve to Sealing position. Press Manual; cook at high pressure 10 minutes.

4. When cooking is complete, press Cancel and use quick release. Remove chicken to clean plate; tent with foil.

5. If thicker sauce is desired, stir flour into water in small bowl until smooth. Press Sauté; add flour mixture to pot and cook about 5 minutes or until sauce thickens, stirring frequently. Serve sauce with chicken; sprinkle with prosciutto.

MAKES 4 SERVINGS

HEARTY CHICKEN CHILI

1 tablespoon vegetable oil

1 onion, finely chopped

1 jalapeño pepper, minced

1 clove garlic, minced

1½ teaspoons chili powder

¾ teaspoon salt

½ teaspoon ground cumin

½ teaspoon dried oregano

½ teaspoon black pepper

¼ teaspoon red pepper flakes (optional)

1 cup chicken broth

1½ pounds boneless skinless chicken thighs, cut into 1-inch pieces

2 cans (about 15 ounces each) hominy, rinsed and drained

1 can (about 15 ounces) pinto beans, rinsed and drained

1 tablespoon all-purpose flour (optional)

Chopped fresh cilantro (optional)

1. Press Sauté; heat oil in Instant Pot®. Add onion; cook and stir 3 minutes or until softened. Add jalapeño, garlic, chili powder, salt, cumin, oregano, black pepper and red pepper flakes, if desired; cook and stir 30 seconds. Stir in broth; cook 1 minute. Add chicken, hominy and beans; mix well.

2. Secure lid and move pressure release valve to Sealing position. Press Manual; cook at high pressure 6 minutes.

3. When cooking is complete, use natural release for 10 minutes, then release remaining pressure.

4. For thicker chili, stir 1 tablespoon flour into 3 tablespoons cooking liquid in small bowl until smooth. Press Sauté; add flour mixture to chili. Cook about 5 minutes or until chili thickens, stirring occasionally. Garnish with cilantro.

MAKES 4 SERVINGS

HOISIN BARBECUE CHICKEN SLIDERS

⅔ cup hoisin sauce

⅓ cup barbecue sauce

1 tablespoon soy sauce

¼ teaspoon red pepper flakes

3 to 3½ pounds boneless, skinless chicken thighs

2 tablespoons water

1 tablespoon cornstarch

16 dinner rolls or Hawaiian sweet rolls, split

½ medium red onion, finely chopped

Sliced pickles (optional)

1. Combine hoisin sauce, barbecue sauce, soy sauce and red pepper flakes in Instant Pot®; mix well. Add chicken; stir to coat.

2. Secure lid and move pressure release valve to Sealing position. Press Manual; cook at high pressure 8 minutes.

3. When cooking is complete, use natural release for 5 minutes, then release remaining pressure. Remove chicken to plate; let stand until cool enough to handle. Shred chicken into bite-size pieces.

4. Stir water into cornstarch in small bowl until smooth. Press Sauté; add cornstarch mixture to pot. Cook and stir about 2 minutes or until sauce thickens. Return chicken to pot; mix well. Spoon about ¼ cup chicken onto each roll; serve with onion and pickles, if desired.

MAKES 16 SLIDERS

SPANISH CHICKEN AND RICE

2 tablespoons olive oil

1 package (about 12 ounces) kielbasa sausage, cut into ½-inch slices

2 pounds boneless skinless chicken thighs (about 6)

1 onion, chopped

4 cloves garlic, minced

2 cups uncooked converted long grain rice

1 red bell pepper, diced

½ cup diced carrots

¾ teaspoon salt

¼ teaspoon black pepper

¼ teaspoon saffron threads (optional)

3 cups chicken broth

½ cup thawed frozen peas

1. Press Sauté; heat oil in Instant Pot®. Add sausage; cook about 6 minutes or until browned. Remove to plate. Add chicken to pot in two batches; cook about 8 minutes or until browned on both sides. Remove to plate.

2. Add onion to pot; cook and stir 3 minutes or until softened. Add garlic; cook and stir 30 seconds. Add rice, bell pepper, carrots, salt, black pepper and saffron, if desired; cook and stir 3 minutes. Stir in broth, scraping up browned bits from bottom of pot. Return chicken and sausage to pot, pressing chicken into liquid.

3. Secure lid and move pressure release valve to Sealing position. Press Manual; cook at high pressure 7 minutes.

4. When cooking is complete, press Cancel and use quick release. Remove chicken to clean plate; tent with foil.

5. Stir in peas; let stand 2 minutes or until peas are heated through.

MAKES 6 SERVINGS

THAI PUMPKIN CHICKEN SOUP

1 tablespoon vegetable oil

1 pound boneless skinless chicken breasts, cut into 1-inch pieces

1 white onion, thinly sliced

2 stalks celery, diced

2 carrots, diced

1 tablespoon minced garlic

1 tablespoon minced fresh ginger

½ teaspoon salt

¼ to ½ teaspoon red pepper flakes

2 cups chicken broth

1 cup canned pumpkin

½ cup creamy peanut butter

½ cup minced fresh cilantro, divided

2 tablespoons rice vinegar

1 tablespoon cornstarch

2 tablespoons lime juice

Hot cooked jasmine or basmati rice

2 green onions, minced

½ cup roasted unsalted peanuts, coarsely chopped

Lime wedges (optional)

1. Press Sauté; heat oil in Instant Pot®. Add chicken; cook and stir 5 minutes or until no longer pink. Add onion, celery, carrots, garlic, ginger, salt and red pepper flakes to pot; cook and stir 5 minutes or until vegetables begin to soften. Stir in broth, pumpkin, peanut butter, ¼ cup cilantro and vinegar; mix well.

2. Secure lid and move pressure release valve to Sealing position. Press Manual; cook at high pressure 5 minutes.

3. When cooking is complete, use natural release for 10 minutes, then release remaining pressure.

4. Stir ¼ cup hot soup into cornstarch in small bowl until smooth. Press Sauté; add cornstarch mixture to pot. Cook and stir 2 to 3 minutes or until soup thickens. Stir in lime juice. Serve soup with rice, remaining ¼ cup cilantro, green onions, peanuts and lime wedges, if desired.

MAKES 6 SERVINGS

INDIAN-STYLE APRICOT CHICKEN

2½ pounds bone-in skinless chicken thighs (about 6)

½ teaspoon salt

¼ teaspoon black pepper

1 tablespoon vegetable oil

1 large onion, chopped

½ cup chicken broth, divided

1 tablespoon grated fresh ginger

2 cloves garlic, minced

½ teaspoon ground cinnamon

⅛ teaspoon ground allspice

1 can (about 14 ounces) diced tomatoes

1 package (8 ounces) dried apricots

Pinch saffron threads (optional)

Hot cooked basmati rice (optional)

Chopped fresh Italian parsley (optional)

1. Season both sides of chicken with ½ teaspoon salt and ¼ teaspoon pepper. Press Sauté; heat oil in Instant Pot®. Add chicken in two batches; cook about 8 minutes or until browned on both sides. Remove to plate.

2. Add onion and 2 tablespoons broth to pot; cook and stir 5 minutes or until onion is translucent, scraping up browned bits from bottom of pot. Add ginger, garlic, cinnamon and allspice; cook and stir 30 seconds or until fragrant. Stir in tomatoes, apricots, remaining broth and saffron, if desired; mix well. Return chicken to pot, pressing into liquid.

3. Secure lid and move pressure release valve to Sealing position. Press Manual; cook at high pressure 11 minutes.

4. When cooking is complete, press Cancel and use quick release. Season with additional salt and pepper. Serve with rice, if desired. Garnish with parsley.

MAKES 4 TO 6 SERVINGS

PROVENÇAL LEMON AND OLIVE CHICKEN

2 cups chopped onions

2½ pounds bone-in skinless chicken thighs (about 6)

1 lemon, thinly sliced and seeded

1 cup pitted green olives

1 tablespoon olive brine or white vinegar

2 teaspoons herbes de Provence*

1 bay leaf

1 teaspoon salt

¼ teaspoon black pepper

⅓ cup chicken broth

½ cup minced fresh Italian parsley

*Or substitute ½ teaspoon each dried rosemary, thyme, sage and savory.

1. Place onions in Instant Pot®. Arrange chicken over onions; top with lemon slices. Add olives, brine, herbes de Provence, bay leaf, salt and pepper. Pour in broth.

2. Secure lid and move pressure release valve to Sealing position. Press Manual; cook at high pressure 10 minutes.

3. When cooking is complete, press Cancel and use quick release. Remove chicken to plate; tent with foil.

4. Press Sauté; cook about 5 minutes or until sauce is reduced by one third. Remove and discard bay leaf; stir in parsley. Serve sauce with chicken.

MAKES 4 SERVINGS

CHICKEN ENCHILADA CHILI

1 can (about 14 ounces) diced tomatoes with green chiles

1 can (10 ounces) red enchilada sauce

½ teaspoon salt

¼ teaspoon ground cumin

⅛ teaspoon black pepper

1½ pounds boneless skinless chicken thighs, cut into 1-inch pieces

1 cup frozen or canned corn

1½ tablespoons cornmeal

2 tablespoons finely chopped fresh cilantro

½ cup (2 ounces) shredded pepper jack cheese

Sliced green onions (optional)

1. Combine tomatoes, enchilada sauce, salt, cumin and pepper in Instant Pot®; mix well. Add chicken; stir to coat.

2. Secure lid and move pressure release valve to Sealing position. Press Manual; cook at high pressure 5 minutes.

3. When cooking is complete, use natural release for 10 minutes, then release remaining pressure.

4. Press Sauté; add corn and cornmeal to pot. Cook about 6 minutes or until chili thickens, stirring frequently. Stir in cilantro. Sprinkle with cheese; garnish with green onions.

MAKES 4 SERVINGS

AUTUMN CHICKEN AND VEGETABLES

3 to 4 pounds bone-in chicken thighs

½ teaspoon salt

½ teaspoon black pepper

½ cup all-purpose flour

2 tablespoons olive oil

½ cup apple cider or juice

¼ cup chicken broth

1 teaspoon dried thyme

1 small butternut squash, cut into ¾-inch pieces (about 4 cups)

1 bulb fennel, thinly sliced

½ cup walnuts (optional)

¼ cup fresh basil leaves, very thinly sliced (optional)

1. Season chicken with salt and pepper; coat lightly with flour. Press Sauté; heat oil in Instant Pot®. Add chicken in two batches; cook about 8 minutes or until browned on both sides. Remove to plate. Stir in cider, broth and thyme; cook 1 minute, scraping up browned bits from bottom of pot. Return chicken to pot, pressing into liquid.

2. Secure lid and move pressure release valve to Sealing position. Press Manual; cook at high pressure 6 minutes.

3. When cooking is complete, press Cancel and use quick release.

4. Add squash and fennel to pot. Secure lid and move pressure release valve to Sealing position. Press Manual; cook at high pressure 3 minutes.

5. When cooking is complete, press Cancel and use quick release. Remove chicken and vegetables to plate; keep warm.

6. Press Sauté; cook about 5 minutes or until sauce is reduced by one third and thickens slightly. Serve sauce with chicken and vegetables; sprinkle with walnuts and basil, if desired.

MAKES 6 SERVINGS

CHICKEN ORZO SOUP

1 tablespoon
   vegetable oil

1 onion, chopped

1 bulb fennel,
   quartered, cored
   and thinly sliced
   (reserve fronds
   for garnish)

2 teaspoons minced
   garlic

6 cups chicken broth

1½ pounds boneless
   skinless chicken
   breasts

2 carrots, peeled
   and cut into
   ¼-inch slices

2 sprigs fresh thyme

1 bay leaf

¾ teaspoon salt

¼ teaspoon black
   pepper

½ cup uncooked orzo

1. Press Sauté; heat oil in Instant Pot®. Add onion and fennel; cook and stir about 6 minutes or until tender. Add garlic; cook and stir 1 minute. Add broth, chicken, carrots, thyme, bay leaf, salt and pepper; mix well.

2. Secure lid and move pressure release valve to Sealing position. Press Manual; cook at high pressure 9 minutes.

3. When cooking is complete, use natural release for 10 minutes, then release remaining pressure. Remove chicken to plate; let stand until cool enough to handle.

4. Meanwhile, press Sauté; add orzo to pot. Cook about 10 minutes or until orzo is tender. Remove and discard thyme sprigs and bay leaf.

5. Shred chicken into bite-size pieces. Return chicken to pot; mix well. Garnish soup with fennel fronds.

MAKES 6 TO 8 SERVINGS

ITALIAN COUNTRY-STYLE CHICKEN

½ cup dried porcini
   mushrooms
   (about ½ ounce)

1 cup boiling water

⅓ cup all-purpose flour

1 teaspoon salt

½ teaspoon black pepper

1 cut-up whole chicken
   (3½ to 4 pounds)*

2 tablespoons olive oil

1 medium onion, chopped

2 carrots, cut diagonally
   into ¼-inch slices

3 ounces pancetta,**
   chopped (about ½ cup)

3 cloves garlic, minced

1 tablespoon tomato paste

1 cup pitted green Italian
   olives

*Or use 2 leg quarters and
2 breasts and cut each into
two pieces.*

**Or substitute 3 ounces bacon.*

1. Place mushrooms in small bowl; cover with boiling water. Let stand 15 to 20 minutes or until softened.

2. Meanwhile, combine flour, 1 teaspoon salt and ½ teaspoon pepper in large resealable food storage bag. Add 1 or 2 pieces of chicken at a time; toss to coat. Shake off any excess flour mixture.

3. Press Sauté; heat oil in Instant Pot®. Add chicken in two batches; cook about 8 minutes or until browned on all sides. Remove to plate. Pour off all but 1 tablespoon fat.

4. Drain mushrooms; strain and reserve soaking liquid. Chop mushrooms. Add onion, carrots and pancetta to pot; cook and stir 5 minutes. Add garlic and tomato paste; cook and stir 1 minute. Add reserved mushroom liquid; cook 2 minutes, scraping up browned bits from bottom of pot. Stir in mushrooms; mix well. Return chicken to pot, pressing into liquid.

5. Secure lid and move pressure release valve to Sealing position. Press Manual; cook at high pressure 10 minutes.

6. When cooking is complete, press Cancel and use quick release. Remove chicken to platter; tent with foil.

7. Press Sauté. Add olives; cook about 2 minutes or until heated through and sauce thickens slightly, stirring frequently. Season with additional salt and pepper, if desired. Pour sauce over chicken.

MAKES 4 SERVINGS

BRAISED CHICKEN WITH VEGETABLES

¾ cup chicken broth

2 tablespoons lemon juice

2 cloves garlic, minced

1½ teaspoons Italian seasoning

¾ teaspoon cornstarch

½ teaspoon salt

½ teaspoon dried rosemary

½ teaspoon paprika

¼ teaspoon black pepper

4 chicken drumsticks, skin removed

1 yellow squash, cut into ½-inch pieces

1 zucchini, cut into ½-inch pieces

1 onion, cut into ½-inch pieces

1 small red bell pepper, cut into ½-inch pieces

1. Combine broth, lemon juice, garlic, Italian seasoning, cornstarch, salt, rosemary, paprika and black pepper in Instant Pot®; mix well. Add chicken; stir to coat.

2. Secure lid and move pressure release valve to Sealing position. Press Manual; cook at high pressure 10 minutes.

3. When cooking is complete, press Cancel and use quick release.

4. Add squash, zucchini, onion and bell pepper to pot; press into cooking liquid. Press Manual; cook at high pressure 1 minute. When cooking is complete, press Cancel and use quick release. Remove chicken and vegetables to platter with slotted spoon; tent with foil.

5. Press Sauté; cook about 5 minutes or until sauce is slightly reduced. Serve sauce over chicken and vegetables.

MAKES 2 TO 4 SERVINGS

CHINESE CHICKEN STEW

1 pound boneless skinless chicken thighs, cut into 1-inch pieces

1 teaspoon Chinese five-spice powder

½ teaspoon red pepper flakes

¼ teaspoon salt

1 tablespoon peanut or vegetable oil

1 onion, coarsely chopped

1 package (8 ounces) mushrooms, sliced

2 cloves garlic, minced

⅓ cup plus 2 tablespoons chicken broth, divided

1 tablespoon plus 1 teaspoon soy sauce, divided

1 red bell pepper, cut into ½-inch pieces

2 green onions, cut into ½-inch pieces

1 tablespoon cornstarch

1 teaspoon dark sesame oil

Hot cooked rice

¼ cup coarsely chopped fresh cilantro (optional)

1. Combine chicken, five-spice powder, red pepper flakes and salt in medium bowl; toss to coat. Press Sauté; heat peanut oil in Instant Pot®. Add onion and chicken; cook and stir 5 minutes or until chicken is browned. Add mushrooms and garlic; cook and stir 3 minutes, scraping up browned bits from bottom of pot. Stir in ⅓ cup broth and 1 teaspoon soy sauce; mix well.

2. Secure lid and move pressure release valve to Sealing position. Press Manual; cook at high pressure 5 minutes.

3. When cooking is complete, press Cancel and use quick release.

4. Press Sauté; add bell pepper and green onions to pot. Cook 3 minutes, stirring occasionally. Stir remaining 2 tablespoons broth into cornstarch in small bowl until smooth. Add cornstarch mixture to pot with remaining 1 tablespoon soy sauce and sesame oil; cook and stir 2 minutes or until sauce thickens. Serve stew with rice; sprinkle with cilantro, if desired.

MAKES 4 SERVINGS

8 cups water

1 onion, cut into quarters

1 clove garlic, cut in half

1 bay leaf

3 sprigs fresh parsley

½ teaspoon salt

3 whole black peppercorns

2 pounds bone-in chicken pieces (wings, backs and/or leg quarters, cut up)

1. Combine water, onion, garlic, bay leaf, parsley, salt and peppercorns in Instant Pot®; mix well. Add chicken to pot.

2. Secure lid and move pressure release valve to Sealing position. Press Manual; cook at high pressure 60 minutes.

3. When cooking is complete, use natural release.

4. Strain stock into large bowl through fine-mesh strainer or colander lined with several layers of damp cheesecloth. If there is meat remaining after cooking, set aside for soup or other recipes calling for cooked chicken; discard remaining solids. To remove fat, cover and refrigerate stock overnight; fat will rise to the top and can be easily skimmed off the next day. Stock can be refrigerated up to 3 days or frozen up to 3 months.

MAKES ABOUT 8 CUPS

CLASSIC DEVILED EGGS

1 cup water

6 eggs

Ice water

3 tablespoons mayonnaise

1 tablespoon minced
   fresh dill *or* 1 teaspoon
   dried dill weed

1 tablespoon minced
   dill pickle (optional)

1 teaspoon Dijon mustard

¼ teaspoon salt

⅛ teaspoon white pepper

Paprika (optional)

Fresh dill sprigs (optional)

1. Pour 1 cup water into Instant Pot®. Place rack in pot; place eggs on rack (or use steamer basket to hold eggs).

2. Secure lid and move pressure release valve to Sealing position. Press Manual; cook at low pressure 9 minutes.

3. When cooking is complete, press Cancel and use quick release. Immediately remove eggs to bowl of ice water; let cool 5 to 10 minutes.

4. Peel eggs; cut in half lengthwise. Transfer yolks to small bowl. Add mayonnaise, minced dill, pickle, if desired, mustard, salt and pepper; mash with fork until well blended.

5. Fill egg halves with yolk mixture using teaspoon or piping bag fitted with large plain tip. Garnish with paprika and dill sprigs.

MAKES 6 SERVINGS

TIPS: You can use this method to cook 3 to 12 eggs. If you don't need to use the eggs right away, store them unpeeled in the refrigerator for up to 1 week. For soft-boiled eggs, cook at low pressure 3 to 4 minutes. For eggs in between soft and hard-cooked, cook at low pressure 5 to 7 minutes. Remove to a bowl of ice water after cooking as directed above.

MUSTARD, GARLIC AND HERB TURKEY BREAST

1 tablespoon
vegetable oil

1 bone-in turkey
breast (about
3½ pounds),
skin removed

2 tablespoons spicy
brown mustard

2 tablespoons
chopped fresh
parsley

1 tablespoon
chopped fresh
thyme *or*
1 teaspoon
dried thyme

1 tablespoon
chopped fresh
sage *or* 1 teaspoon
dried sage

1 clove garlic, minced

1 teaspoon salt

½ teaspoon black
pepper

1½ cups water

¼ cup all-purpose
flour (optional)

1. Press Sauté; heat oil in Instant Pot®. Add turkey; cook about 10 minutes or until browned on all sides.

2. Meanwhile, combine mustard, parsley, thyme, sage, garlic, salt and pepper in small bowl; mix well. Remove turkey from pot; rub herb mixture over turkey. Pour water into pot. Place rack in pot; place turkey on rack.

3. Secure lid and move pressure release valve to Sealing position. Press Manual; cook at high pressure 30 minutes.

4. When cooking is complete, use natural release for 10 minutes, then release remaining pressure. Remove turkey to cutting board; tent with foil. Let stand 10 minutes before slicing.

5. If desired, prepare gravy with cooking liquid. Stir ½ cup cooking liquid into flour in small bowl until smooth. Press Sauté; add flour mixture to pot. Cook 5 minutes or until gravy thickens, stirring frequently.

MAKES 4 TO 6 SERVINGS

CUBAN-STYLE CURRIED TURKEY

2 tablespoons all-purpose
  flour

1 teaspoon salt

¼ teaspoon black pepper

1 pound boneless turkey
  breast meat or turkey
  tenderloins, cut into
  1-inch pieces

2 tablespoons vegetable oil,
  divided

1 onion, chopped

½ cup chicken broth,
  divided

1 clove garlic, minced

½ teaspoon curry powder

⅛ teaspoon red pepper
  flakes

1 can (about 15 ounces)
  black beans, rinsed
  and drained

1 can (about 14 ounces)
  diced tomatoes

⅓ cup raisins

1 tablespoon lime juice

1 tablespoon minced
  fresh cilantro (optional)

1 tablespoon minced
  green onion (optional)

  Hot cooked rice (optional)

1. Combine flour, salt and black pepper in large resealable food storage bag. Add turkey; toss to coat. Shake off any excess flour mixture. Press Sauté; heat 1 tablespoon oil in Instant Pot®. Add turkey; cook about 5 minutes or until browned. Remove to plate.

2. Add remaining 1 tablespoon oil, onion and ¼ cup broth to pot; cook and stir 3 minutes, scraping up browned bits from bottom of pot. Add garlic, curry powder and red pepper flakes; cook and stir 30 seconds. Stir in beans, tomatoes, raisins and remaining ¼ cup broth; mix well.

3. Secure lid and move pressure release valve to Sealing position. Press Manual; cook at high pressure 5 minutes.

4. When cooking is complete, press Cancel and use quick release.

5. Press Sauté; cook 3 minutes or until sauce is reduced and thickens slightly. Stir in lime juice; garnish with cilantro and green onion. Serve over rice, if desired.

MAKES 4 SERVINGS

BARBECUE TURKEY DRUMSTICKS

⅓ cup white vinegar

⅓ cup ketchup

⅓ cup molasses

2 tablespoons Worcestershire sauce

2 teaspoons onion powder

2 teaspoons garlic powder

¾ teaspoon liquid smoke

⅛ teaspoon chipotle chili powder

4 turkey drumsticks (8 to 12 ounces each)

1¼ teaspoons salt

1¼ teaspoons black pepper

1. Combine vinegar, ketchup, molasses, Worcestershire sauce, onion powder, garlic powder, liquid smoke and chipotle chili powder in measuring cup or medium bowl; mix well.

2. Season drumsticks with salt and pepper; place in Instant Pot®. Pour sauce over drumsticks, turning to coat completely.

3. Secure lid and move pressure release valve to Sealing position. Press Manual; cook at high pressure 35 minutes.

4. When cooking is complete, use natural release. Remove drumsticks from pot; let stand 10 minutes before serving. Serve with remaining sauce.

MAKES 4 SERVINGS

TURKEY NOODLE SOUP

1 tablespoon olive oil

1 onion, chopped

3 carrots, sliced

3 stalks celery, sliced

2 cloves garlic, minced

1 teaspoon poultry
seasoning

2 turkey drumsticks
(8 to 12 ounces each)

4 cups chicken broth

2 cups water

½ teaspoon salt

6 ounces uncooked
egg noodles

⅓ cup chopped fresh
Italian parsley

Black pepper

1. Press Sauté; heat oil in Instant Pot®. Add onion; cook and stir 3 minutes or until softened. Add carrots, celery, garlic and poultry seasoning; cook and stir 3 minutes. Add drumsticks, broth, water and ½ teaspoon salt.

2. Secure lid and move pressure release valve to Sealing position. Press Manual; cook at high pressure 35 minutes.

3. When cooking is complete, use natural release for 10 minutes, then release remaining pressure. Remove turkey to plate; set aside 10 minutes or until cool enough to handle.

4. Meanwhile, press Sauté; bring soup to a boil. Add noodles to pot; cook 8 minutes or until tender, stirring occasionally.

5. Remove and discard skin and bones from turkey; shred meat into bite-size pieces. Stir turkey and parsley into soup; cook until heated through. Season with additional salt and pepper.

MAKES 6 SERVINGS

1 tablespoon olive oil

1 onion, thinly sliced

1 green bell pepper, chopped

1 clove garlic, minced

¾ teaspoon ground cumin

½ teaspoon dried oregano

2 medium tomatoes, chopped

1 can (8 ounces) tomato sauce

⅓ cup sliced pimiento-stuffed green olives

½ teaspoon salt

¼ teaspoon black pepper

1 pound turkey tenderloins (2 large or 3 small) *or* 1½ pounds boneless turkey breast, cut into 3 to 4 pieces

1 tablespoon lemon juice

Hot cooked rice and beans (optional)

1. Press Sauté; heat oil in Instant Pot®. Add onion and bell pepper; cook and stir 3 minutes or until softened. Add garlic, cumin and oregano; cook and stir 30 seconds. Stir in tomatoes, tomato sauce, olives, salt and black pepper; mix well. Add turkey to pot, pressing into tomato mixture.

2. Secure lid and move pressure release valve to Sealing position. Press Manual; cook at high pressure 20 minutes.

3. When cooking is complete, use natural release for 10 minutes, then release remaining pressure. Remove turkey to plate.

4. Press Sauté; cook 10 to 15 minutes or until sauce is reduced by one third.

5. Meanwhile, shred turkey into bite-size pieces when cool enough to handle. Add shredded turkey and lemon juice to sauce; mix well. Serve with rice and beans, if desired.

MAKES 4 SERVINGS

CHILI TURKEY BREAST WITH CILANTRO-LIME RICE

TURKEY

- 1½ tablespoons chili powder
- 2 teaspoons dried oregano
- 1½ teaspoons ground cumin
- ½ teaspoon red pepper flakes
- ½ teaspoon salt
- ½ teaspoon black pepper
- 1 bone-in turkey breast (about 3½ pounds), skin removed
- 1 cup chicken broth

RICE

- 1½ cups long grain rice
- ¾ cup water
- 2 medium red bell peppers, chopped
- 1 cup chopped green onions
- ½ cup chopped fresh cilantro
- 2 tablespoons lime juice
- 1 tablespoon grated lime peel
- 1 tablespoon olive oil
- ½ teaspoon ground turmeric (optional)
- ¼ teaspoon salt

1. Combine chili powder, oregano, cumin, red pepper flakes, salt and black pepper in small bowl; mix well. Rub into all sides of turkey. Pour broth into Instant Pot®. Place rack in pot; place turkey on rack.

2. Secure lid and move pressure release valve to Sealing position. Press Manual; cook at high pressure 35 minutes.

3. When cooking is complete, use natural release for 10 minutes, then release remaining pressure. Remove turkey to cutting board; tent with foil. Reserve ¾ cup cooking liquid for rice; discard remaining liquid. Wipe out pot with paper towels.

4. Rinse rice well; drain in fine-mesh strainer. Combine rice, reserved ¾ cup cooking liquid, water, bell peppers, green onions, cilantro, lime juice, lime peel, oil, turmeric, if desired, and salt in pot; mix well.

5. Secure lid and move pressure release valve to Sealing position. Press Manual; cook at high pressure 4 minutes.

6. When cooking is complete, use natural release for 10 minutes, then release remaining pressure. Fluff rice gently with fork before serving with turkey.

MAKES 6 TO 8 SERVINGS

TURKEY STROGANOFF

1 tablespoon olive oil

4 cups sliced mushrooms

2 stalks celery, sliced

2 medium shallots *or* ½ small onion, minced

2 turkey tenderloins (about 10 ounces each) or turkey breast meat, cut into 1-inch pieces

¼ cup chicken broth

1½ tablespoons Worcestershire sauce

¾ teaspoon salt

½ teaspoon dried thyme

¼ teaspoon black pepper

½ cup sour cream

1 tablespoon all-purpose flour

Hot cooked egg noodles

1. Press Sauté; heat oil in Instant Pot®. Add mushrooms, celery and shallots; cook and stir 5 minutes or until vegetables are tender. Add turkey, broth, Worcestershire sauce, salt, thyme and pepper; mix well.

2. Secure lid and move pressure release valve to Sealing position. Press Manual; cook at high pressure 6 minutes.

3. When cooking is complete, use natural release for 5 minutes, then release remaining pressure.

4. Combine sour cream and flour in small bowl; stir in ¼ cup hot cooking liquid from pot until smooth. Press Sauté; add sour cream mixture to pot. Cook and stir 3 minutes or until sauce thickens. Serve over noodles.

MAKES 4 SERVINGS

TURKEY MEATBALLS WITH CRANBERRY BARBECUE SAUCE

1 egg

1 pound ground turkey

⅓ cup plain dry bread crumbs

1 green onion, finely chopped

1 tablespoon soy sauce

2 teaspoons grated orange peel

½ teaspoon salt, divided

¼ teaspoon black pepper

¼ teaspoon ground red pepper

1 can (16 ounces) jellied cranberry sauce

½ cup barbecue sauce

1. Beat egg in medium bowl. Add turkey, bread crumbs, green onion, soy sauce, orange peel, ¼ teaspoon salt, black pepper and red pepper; mix gently until blended. Shape into 24 balls.

2. Combine cranberry sauce, barbecue sauce and remaining ¼ teaspoon salt in large microwavable bowl. Cover and microwave on HIGH 4 minutes or until cranberry sauce is melted and mixture is heated through, stirring after 2 minutes.

3. Spray Instant Pot® with nonstick cooking spray; place meatballs in pot. Pour cranberry sauce mixture over meatballs.

4. Secure lid and move pressure release valve to Sealing position. Press Manual; cook at high pressure 7 minutes.

5. When cooking is complete, use natural release for 5 minutes, then release remaining pressure. Press Sauté; adjust heat to low ("less"). Cook about 8 minutes or until sauce is reduced and thickens slightly.

MAKES 6 TO 8 SERVINGS

MU SHU TURKEY

1 jar (about 7 ounces) plum sauce, divided

¼ cup orange juice (juice of 1 medium orange)

¼ cup finely chopped onion

1 tablespoon minced fresh ginger

¼ teaspoon salt

¼ teaspoon ground cinnamon

1 pound boneless turkey breast, cut into thin strips

6 (7-inch) flour tortillas

3 cups coleslaw mix

1. Combine ⅓ cup plum sauce, orange juice, onion, ginger, salt and cinnamon in Instant Pot®; mix well. Add turkey, stir to coat.

2. Secure lid and move pressure release valve to Sealing position. Press Manual; cook at high pressure 4 minutes.

3. When cooking is complete, press Cancel and use quick release.

4. Press Sauté; cook 2 to 3 minutes or until sauce is reduced and thickens slightly.

5. Spread remaining jarred plum sauce over tortillas; top with turkey and coleslaw mix. Fold bottom edge of tortillas over filling; fold in sides and roll up to completely enclose filling. Serve with remaining cooking sauce for dipping.

MAKES 6 SERVINGS

HERB LEMON TURKEY BREAST

½ cup lemon juice

½ cup dry white wine

4 cloves garlic, minced

1 teaspoon salt

½ teaspoon dried parsley flakes

½ teaspoon dried tarragon

½ teaspoon dried rosemary

¼ teaspoon ground sage

¼ teaspoon black pepper

1 bone-in turkey breast (about 3½ pounds)

Fresh herbs and lemon slices (optional)

1. Combine lemon juice, wine, garlic, salt, parsley flakes, tarragon, dried rosemary, sage and pepper in measuring cup or small bowl; mix well.

2. Place turkey breast in Instant Pot®; pour juice mixture over turkey, turning to coat. (Turkey should be right side up for cooking.)

3. Secure lid and move pressure release valve to Sealing position. Press Manual; cook at high pressure 30 minutes.

4. When cooking is complete, use natural release for 10 minutes, then release remaining pressure. Remove turkey to cutting board; tent with foil. Let stand 10 minutes before slicing.

5. Use cooking liquid as sauce, if desired, or thicken liquid with flour (see Tip). Garnish as desired.

MAKES 4 SERVINGS

TIP: If desired, prepare gravy with cooking liquid after removing turkey from pot. Place ¼ cup all-purpose flour in small bowl; stir in ½ cup hot cooking liquid until smooth. Press Sauté; add flour mixture to pot. Cook 5 minutes or until gravy thickens, stirring frequently.

SPICY PEANUT TURKEY

1½ pounds turkey tenderloins, cut into ¾-inch pieces

½ cup plus 2 tablespoons chicken broth, divided

2 tablespoons soy sauce

3 cloves garlic, minced

½ teaspoon red pepper flakes

¼ teaspoon salt

1 red bell pepper, cut into short, thin strips

3 green onions, cut into ½-inch pieces

⅓ cup creamy or chunky peanut butter (not natural-style)

1 tablespoon cornstarch

⅓ cup roasted peanuts, chopped

⅓ cup chopped fresh cilantro

Hot cooked rice noodles or egg noodles (optional)

1. Combine turkey, ½ cup broth, soy sauce, garlic, red pepper flakes and salt in Instant Pot®; mix well.

2. Secure lid and move pressure release valve to Sealing position. Press Manual; cook at high pressure 5 minutes.

3. When cooking is complete, press Cancel and use quick release.

4. Press Sauté; add bell pepper, green onions and peanut butter to pot. Cook 3 minutes or until bell pepper is crisp-tender, stirring frequently.

5. Stir remaining 2 tablespoons broth into cornstarch in small bowl until smooth. Add cornstarch mixture to pot; cook 2 minutes or until sauce thickens, stirring constantly. Sprinkle with peanuts and cilantro; serve over noodles, if desired.

MAKES 4 TO 6 SERVINGS

SEA BASS WITH VEGETABLES

2 tablespoons butter
  or olive oil

2 bulbs fennel, thinly sliced

3 large carrots, julienned

3 large leeks, thinly sliced

¾ teaspoon salt, divided

¼ teaspoon plus ⅛ teaspoon
  black pepper, divided

6 sea bass fillets or other
  firm-fleshed white fish
  (6 to 8 ounces each)

¼ cup water

1. Press Sauté; melt butter in Instant Pot®. Add fennel, carrots and leeks; cook about 8 minutes or until vegetables are softened and beginning to brown, stirring occasionally. Stir in ½ teaspoon salt and ¼ teaspoon pepper. Remove half of vegetables to plate.

2. Season sea bass with remaining ¼ teaspoon salt and ⅛ teaspoon pepper; place on top of vegetables in pot. Top with remaining vegetables. Drizzle with water.

3. Secure lid and move pressure release valve to Sealing position. Press Manual; cook at low pressure 4 minutes.

4. When cooking is complete, press Cancel and use quick release. Serve sea bass with vegetables.

MAKES 6 SERVINGS

SHRIMP AND OKRA GUMBO

1 tablespoon olive oil

8 ounces kielbasa, halved lengthwise then cut crosswise into ¼-inch slices

1 green bell pepper, chopped

1 medium onion, chopped

3 stalks celery, cut into ¼-inch slices

6 green onions, chopped

4 cloves garlic, minced

1 can (about 14 ounces) diced tomatoes

½ cup chicken broth

1 teaspoon Cajun seasoning

½ teaspoon dried thyme

¼ teaspoon salt

2 cups frozen cut okra, thawed

1 pound large raw shrimp, peeled and deveined (with tails on)

1. Press Sauté; heat oil in Instant Pot®. Add kielbasa; cook and stir 4 minutes or until browned. Remove to plate.

2. Add bell pepper, chopped onion, celery, green onions and garlic to pot; cook and stir 6 minutes or until vegetables are softened. Stir in tomatoes, broth, Cajun seasoning, thyme and salt; mix well.

3. Secure lid and move pressure release valve to Sealing position. Press Manual; cook at high pressure 4 minutes.

4. When cooking is complete, press Cancel and use quick release.

5. Add okra to pot. Secure lid and move pressure release valve to Sealing position. Press Manual; cook at high pressure 1 minute. When cooking is complete, press Cancel and use quick release.

6. Press Sauté; add shrimp to pot. Cook 2 to 3 minutes or until shrimp are pink and opaque, stirring occasionally.

MAKES 6 SERVINGS

NEW ENGLAND FISH CHOWDER

4 slices bacon, chopped

1 cup chopped onion

½ cup chopped celery

2 cups plus 2 tablespoons water, divided

2 cups peeled russet potatoes, cut into 1-inch pieces

1 teaspoon dried dill weed

½ teaspoon dried thyme

½ teaspoon salt

½ teaspoon black pepper

1 bay leaf

1 pound cod, haddock, or halibut fillets, skinned, boned, and cut into 1-inch pieces*

2 tablespoons all-purpose flour

2 cups milk or half-and-half

If fillets are very thin, cut into larger pieces to prevent overcooking.

1. Press Sauté; cook bacon in Instant Pot® until crisp. Remove to paper towel-lined plate.

2. Add onion and celery to pot; cook and stir 3 minutes or until vegetables are softened. Add 2 cups water, potatoes, dill weed, thyme, salt, pepper and bay leaf; mix well.

3. Secure lid and move pressure release valve to Sealing position. Press Manual; cook at high pressure 2 minutes. When cooking is complete, press Cancel and use quick release.

4. Add cod to pot. Secure lid and move pressure release valve to Sealing position. Press Manual; cook at low pressure 1 minute. When cooking is complete, press Cancel and use quick release.

5. Stir remaining 2 tablespoons water into flour in small bowl until smooth. Press Sauté; adjust heat to low ("less"). Add flour mixture to soup; cook and stir 3 minutes or until thickened. Add milk and bacon; cook 2 minutes or until heated through, stirring gently. (Do not boil.) Remove and discard bay leaf.

MAKES 4 TO 6 SERVINGS

SOUTHWESTERN SALMON PO' BOYS

½ teaspoon Southwest seasoning or chipotle chili powder

¼ teaspoon salt

¼ teaspoon black pepper

4 salmon fillets (about 6 ounces each), rinsed and patted dry

1 red bell pepper, thinly sliced

1 green bell pepper, thinly sliced

1 onion, thinly sliced

½ cup Italian vinaigrette dressing

¼ cup water

4 large French or Italian sandwich rolls, split

¼ cup chipotle mayonnaise*

Fresh cilantro leaves (optional)

½ lemon, cut into 4 wedges

*If unavailable, combine ¼ cup mayonnaise with ½ teaspoon adobo sauce. Or substitute regular mayonnaise.

1. Combine Southwest seasoning, salt and black pepper in small bowl; mix well. Rub spice mixture over both sides of salmon.

2. Combine half of bell peppers and half of onion in Instant Pot®. Place salmon on top of vegetables. Pour Italian dressing over salmon; top with remaining bell peppers and onion. Pour water into pot.

3. Secure lid and move pressure release valve to Sealing position. Press Manual; cook at low pressure 4 minutes.

4. When cooking is complete, press Cancel and use quick release. Remove salmon to plate; remove and discard skin.

5. Toast rolls, if desired. Spread top halves with chipotle mayonnaise and cilantro, if desired. Spoon 1 to 2 tablespoons cooking liquid onto bottom halves of rolls; top with warm salmon, vegetable mixture and top halves of rolls. Serve with lemon wedges.

MAKES 4 SERVINGS

ITALIAN FISH SOUP

1 can (about 14 ounces) Italian-seasoned diced tomatoes

1 cup chicken broth

1 small bulb fennel, chopped (about 1 cup), fronds reserved for garnish

3 cloves garlic, minced

1 tablespoon olive oil

½ teaspoon saffron threads, crushed (optional)

½ teaspoon dried basil

¼ teaspoon salt

¼ teaspoon red pepper flakes

8 ounces skinless halibut or cod fillets, cut into 1-inch pieces

8 ounces medium raw shrimp, peeled and deveined

1. Combine tomatoes, broth, chopped fennel, garlic, oil, saffron, if desired, basil, salt and red pepper flakes in Instant Pot®; mix well.

2. Secure lid and move pressure release valve to Sealing position. Press Manual; cook at high pressure 3 minutes. When cooking is complete, press Cancel and use quick release.

3. Add halibut to pot. Secure lid and move pressure release valve to Sealing position. Press Manual; cook at low pressure 1 minute.

4. When cooking is complete, press Cancel and use quick release.

5. Press Sauté; add shrimp to pot. Cook 2 to 3 minutes or until shrimp are pink and opaque, stirring occasionally. Garnish with fennel fronds.

MAKES 4 SERVINGS

COD WITH TAPENADE

Tapenade
(recipe follows)

4 cod fillets or other firm white fish (about 8 ounces each)

¼ teaspoon salt

⅛ teaspoon black pepper

1 cup water

2 lemons, thinly sliced

1. Prepare Tapenade.

2. Season cod with salt and pepper. Pour water into Instant Pot®. Place rack in pot; arrange half of lemon slices on rack. Place fish on lemon slices; top with remaining lemon slices.

3. Secure lid and move pressure release valve to Sealing position. Press Manual; cook at low pressure 2 minutes.

4. When cooking is complete, press Cancel and use quick release. Remove fish to serving plates; discard lemon slices. Serve with Tapenade.

MAKES 4 SERVINGS

TAPENADE

8 ounces pitted kalamata olives

2 tablespoons anchovy paste

2 tablespoons drained capers

2 tablespoons chopped fresh Italian parsley

1 clove garlic

½ teaspoon grated orange peel

⅛ teaspoon ground red pepper

½ cup extra virgin olive oil

Combine olives, anchovy paste, capers, parsley, garlic, orange peel and red pepper in food processor; pulse until coarsely chopped. Add oil; pulse until mixture forms rough paste. (Tapenade should not be completely smooth.)

MAKES ABOUT 1 CUP

TORTILLA SOUP WITH GROUPER

1 tablespoon vegetable oil

1 onion, chopped

2 cloves garlic, minced

3½ cups chicken broth

1 can (about 14 ounces) diced tomatoes

1 can (4 ounces) diced green chiles, drained

2 teaspoons Worcestershire sauce

1 teaspoon salt

1 teaspoon chili powder

1 teaspoon ground cumin

⅛ teaspoon black pepper

1 pound grouper or sole fillets, cut into 1-inch pieces

1 cup frozen corn

3 corn tortillas, cut into 1-inch strips

1. Press Sauté; heat oil in Instant Pot®. Add onion and garlic; cook and stir 3 minutes or until onion is softened. Add broth, tomatoes, chiles, Worcestershire sauce, salt, chili powder, cumin and pepper; mix well.

2. Secure lid and move pressure release valve to Sealing position. Press Manual; cook at high pressure 4 minutes.

3. When cooking is complete, press Cancel and use quick release.

4. Press Sauté; add grouper and corn to pot. Cook about 2 minutes or until fish begins to flake when tested with fork. Stir in tortillas; serve immediately.

MAKES 6 SERVINGS

MISO SALMON

½ cup water

2 green onions, cut into 2-inch pieces

¼ cup yellow miso paste

¼ cup soy sauce

2 tablespoons sake

2 tablespoons mirin

1½ teaspoons grated fresh ginger

1 teaspoon minced garlic

6 salmon fillets (about 4 ounces each)

Hot cooked rice (optional)

Thinly sliced green onions (optional)

1. Combine water, 2 green onions, miso paste, soy sauce, sake, mirin, ginger and garlic in Instant Pot®; mix well. Add salmon to pot, skin side down.

2. Secure lid and move pressure release valve to Sealing position. Press Manual; cook at low pressure 4 minutes.

3. When cooking is complete, press Cancel and use quick release. Serve salmon with rice, if desired. Garnish with sliced green onions; drizzle with cooking liquid.

MAKES 6 SERVINGS

ORZO RISOTTO WITH SHRIMP AND VEGETABLES

1 tablespoon olive oil

1 medium zucchini, halved and sliced

2 teaspoons grated lemon peel

2 cans (about 14 ounces each) chicken broth

1¼ cups uncooked orzo pasta

1 cup sliced mushrooms

½ cup chopped onion

2 cloves garlic, minced

¾ teaspoon salt

¾ teaspoon dried sage

½ teaspoon dried thyme

8 ounces shrimp, peeled and deveined (with tails on)

¾ cup frozen peas, thawed

¼ cup grated Parmesan cheese

Black pepper

1. Press Sauté; heat oil in Instant Pot®. Add zucchini and lemon peel; cook and stir 2 to 3 minutes or until zucchini is tender. Remove to small bowl.

2. Add broth, orzo, mushrooms, onion, garlic, salt, sage and thyme to pot; mix well. Secure lid and move pressure release valve to Sealing position. Press Manual; cook at high pressure 4 minutes.

3. When cooking is complete, press Cancel and use quick release.

4. Press Sauté; adjust heat to low ("less"). Add shrimp and peas; cook about 3 minutes or until shrimp are pink and opaque, stirring frequently. Stir in cheese; season with pepper.

MAKES 4 SERVINGS

SCALLOPS WITH HERB TOMATO SAUCE

2 tablespoons vegetable oil

1 medium red onion, peeled and diced

1 clove garlic, minced

3½ cups fresh tomatoes, peeled*

1 can (6 ounces) tomato paste

¼ cup dry red wine

2 tablespoons chopped fresh Italian parsley

1 tablespoon chopped fresh oregano

1 teaspoon salt

¼ teaspoon black pepper

1½ pounds fresh scallops, cleaned and drained

Hot cooked pasta or rice (optional)

To peel tomatoes, score "x" in bottom of tomatoes and place one at a time in simmering water about 10 seconds. (Add 30 seconds if tomatoes are not fully ripened.) Immediately plunge into bowl of cold water for another 10 seconds. Peel skin with a knife.

1. Press Sauté; heat oil in Instant Pot®. Add onion and garlic; cook and stir 3 to 4 minutes or until onion is soft and translucent. Add tomatoes, tomato paste, wine, parsley, oregano, salt and pepper; mix well.

2. Secure lid and move pressure release valve to Sealing position. Press Manual; cook at high pressure 8 minutes.

3. When cooking is complete, press Cancel and use quick release. Taste sauce; season with additional salt and pepper if necessary.

4. Press Sauté; add scallops to pot. Cook 1 minute or until sauce begins to simmer. Press Cancel; cover pot with lid and let stand 8 minutes or until scallops are opaque. Serve over pasta, if desired.

MAKES 4 SERVINGS

COD CHOWDER

2 tablespoons vegetable oil

1 pound unpeeled red potatoes, diced

2 medium leeks, halved and thinly sliced

2 stalks celery, diced

1 bulb fennel, diced

½ yellow or red bell pepper, diced

2 teaspoons chopped fresh thyme

1¼ teaspoons salt

½ teaspoon black pepper

2 tablespoons all-purpose flour

2 cups clam juice

1 cup water

1½ pounds cod, cut into 1-inch pieces

1 cup frozen corn

1 cup half-and-half

¼ cup finely chopped fresh Italian parsley

1. Press Sauté; heat oil in Instant Pot®. Add potatoes, leeks, celery, fennel, bell pepper, thyme, salt and black pepper; cook about 8 minutes or until vegetables are slightly softened, stirring occasionally. Add flour; cook and stir 1 minute. Add clam juice and water; mix well.

2. Secure lid and move pressure release valve to Sealing position. Press Manual; cook at high pressure 6 minutes.

3. When cooking is complete, press Cancel and use quick release. Use immersion blender to blend soup just until slightly thickened (soup should not be completely smooth).

4. Press Sauté; add cod, corn, half-and-half and parsley to pot. Cook about 2 minutes or until soup begins to simmer and fish is firm and opaque, stirring occasionally.

MAKES 6 TO 8 SERVINGS

QUICK SHRIMP AND OKRA STEW

1 teaspoon vegetable oil

½ cup finely chopped onion

8 ounces okra, ends trimmed, cut into ½-inch slices

1 can (about 14 ounces) whole tomatoes, chopped, juice reserved

1 teaspoon dried thyme

¾ teaspoon salt

8 ounces medium raw shrimp, peeled and deveined

¾ cup fresh corn kernels or thawed frozen corn

½ teaspoon hot pepper sauce

1. Press Sauté; heat oil in Instant Pot®. Add onion; cook and stir 2 minutes or until softened. Add okra; cook and stir 3 minutes. Add tomatoes with juice, thyme and salt; mix well.

2. Secure lid and move pressure release valve to Sealing position. Press Manual; cook at high pressure 4 minutes.

3. When cooking is complete, press Cancel and use quick release.

4. Press Sauté; add shrimp, corn and hot pepper sauce to pot. Cook 3 minutes or until shrimp are pink and opaque, stirring frequently.

MAKES 4 SERVINGS

GREEK-STYLE SALMON

1 tablespoon olive oil

1 can (about 14 ounces) diced tomatoes, drained

¼ cup pitted black olives, coarsely chopped

¼ cup pitted green olives, coarsely chopped

3 tablespoons lemon juice

2 tablespoons chopped fresh Italian parsley

1 tablespoon capers, rinsed and drained

2 cloves garlic, thinly sliced

¼ teaspoon black pepper

1 pound salmon fillets

1. Press Sauté; heat oil in Instant Pot®. Add tomatoes, olives, lemon juice, parsley, capers, garlic and pepper; bring to a simmer, stirring frequently.

2. Secure lid and move pressure release valve to Sealing position. Press Manual; cook at high pressure 4 minutes.

3. When cooking is complete, press Cancel and use quick release.

4. Place salmon in pot, skin side down. Press Sauté; bring to a simmer. Press Cancel; cover pot with lid and let stand 10 minutes or until fish begins to flake when tested with fork.

MAKES 4 SERVINGS

CREAMY CRAB CHOWDER

1 tablespoon butter

1 cup finely chopped onion

2 cloves garlic, minced

1 cup chopped celery

½ cup chopped green bell pepper

½ cup chopped red bell pepper

3 cans (about 14 ounces each) chicken broth

3 cups diced peeled russet potatoes

1 teaspoon salt

½ teaspoon dried thyme

½ teaspoon black pepper

⅛ teaspoon ground red pepper

2 cans (6½ ounces each) lump crabmeat, drained and flaked

1 package (10 ounces) frozen corn

½ cup half-and-half

1. Press Sauté; melt butter in Instant Pot®. Add onion and garlic; cook and stir 3 minutes or until softened. Add celery and bell peppers; cook and stir 4 minutes or until vegetables begin to soften. Stir in broth, potatoes, salt, thyme, black pepper and ground red pepper; mix well.

2. Secure lid and move pressure release valve to Sealing position. Press Manual; cook at high pressure 6 minutes.

3. When cooking is complete, press Cancel and use quick release.

4. Press Sauté; add crabmeat, corn and half-and-half to pot. Cook and stir 2 minutes or until soup begins to simmer.

MAKES 6 TO 8 SERVINGS

SAVORY COD STEW

8 ounces bacon, chopped

1 large onion, diced

1 large carrot, diced

2 stalks celery, diced

2 cloves garlic, minced

1 can (28 ounces) plum tomatoes, coarsely chopped, juice reserved

2 potatoes, peeled and diced

1 cup clam juice

3 tablespoons tomato paste

3 tablespoons chopped fresh Italian parsley

½ teaspoon salt

¼ teaspoon black pepper

3 saffron threads

2½ pounds fresh cod, skin removed, cut into 1½-inch pieces

1. Press Sauté; cook bacon in Instant Pot® until crisp. Drain off all but 2 tablespoons drippings.

2. Add onion, carrot, celery and garlic to pot; cook and stir 5 minutes or until vegetables are softened. Add tomatoes with juice, potatoes, clam juice, tomato paste, parsley, salt, pepper and saffron; cook and stir 2 minutes.

3. Secure lid and move pressure release valve to Sealing position. Press Manual; cook at high pressure 2 minutes.

4. When cooking is complete, press Cancel and use quick release.

5. Add cod to pot. Secure lid and move pressure release valve to Sealing position. Press Manual; cook at low pressure 1 minute.

6. When cooking is complete, press Cancel and use quick release.

MAKES 6 TO 8 SERVINGS

SALMON WITH BOK CHOY

2 tablespoons finely chopped fresh ginger

1 clove garlic, minced

½ cup vegetable broth

3 tablespoons unseasoned rice vinegar

1 tablespoon sugar

1 tablespoon soy sauce

1 teaspoon hoisin sauce

6 cups chopped bok choy

4 (4-ounce) skinless salmon fillets

¼ cup sliced green onions

1. Combine ginger and garlic in small bowl. Combine broth, vinegar, sugar, soy sauce, hoisin sauce and half of ginger mixture in Instant Pot®; mix well. Stir in bok choy.

2. Secure lid and move pressure release valve to Sealing position. Press Manual; cook at high pressure 2 minutes.

3. When cooking is complete, press Cancel and use quick release.

4. Rub remaining ginger mixture over salmon. Place salmon on top of bok choy in pot. Press Sauté; bring liquid to a simmer. Press Cancel; cover pot with lid and let stand 10 minutes. Sprinkle with green onions.

MAKES 4 SERVINGS

SHRIMP JAMBALAYA

2 cans (about 14 ounces each) diced tomatoes, drained

1 medium onion, chopped

1 medium red bell pepper, chopped

1 stalk celery, chopped

2 tablespoons minced garlic

2 teaspoons dried parsley flakes

2 teaspoons dried oregano

1 teaspoon salt

1 teaspoon hot pepper sauce

½ teaspoon dried thyme

2 pounds medium raw shrimp, peeled and deveined

   Hot cooked rice

1. Combine tomatoes, onion, bell pepper, celery, garlic, parsley flakes, oregano, salt, hot pepper sauce and thyme in Instant Pot®; mix well.

2. Secure lid and move pressure release valve to Sealing position. Press Manual; cook at high pressure 9 minutes.

3. When cooking is complete, press Cancel and use quick release.

4. Press Sauté; add shrimp to pot. Cook 5 minutes or until shrimp are pink and opaque and liquid is slightly reduced. Serve over rice.

MAKES 6 SERVINGS

BBQ "Baked" Beans
(page 124)

Cheesy Polenta
(page 144)

**Channa Chat
(Indian-Spiced Snack Mix**
(page 122)

BEANS & GRAINS

**Cheese Grits with
Chiles and Bacon**
(page 108)

Vegetarian Chili
(page 136)

Chicken Congee
(page 134)

Classic Irish Oatmeal
(page 109)

BEANS & GRAINS

FRUITY WHOLE-GRAIN CEREAL

2¼ cups water

¼ cup steel-cut oats

¼ cup uncooked pearled barley

¼ cup uncooked brown rice

½ teaspoon salt

½ cup milk

⅓ cup golden raisins

¼ cup chopped dried dates

¼ cup chopped dried plums

2 tablespoons packed brown sugar

½ teaspoon ground cinnamon

1. Combine water, oats, barley, rice and salt in Instant Pot®; mix well.

2. Secure lid and move pressure release valve to Sealing position. Press Manual; cook at high pressure 20 minutes.

3. When cooking is complete, use natural release for 10 minutes, then release remaining pressure.

4. Stir in milk, raisins, dates, dried plums, brown sugar and cinnamon; mix well. Serve hot. Refrigerate any leftover cereal in airtight container.

MAKES 4 TO 6 SERVINGS

TIP: To reheat cereal, place one serving in a microwavable bowl. Microwave 30 seconds; stir. Add water or milk to reach desired consistency. Microwave just until hot.

WHITE BEANS AND TOMATOES

1 pound dried cannellini
   beans, soaked 8 hours
   or overnight

2 tablespoons olive oil

2 medium onions, chopped

1 tablespoon minced garlic

1 tablespoon tomato paste

4 teaspoons dried oregano

2 teaspoons salt

1 can (28 ounces)
   crushed tomatoes

2 cups water

   Black pepper (optional)

1. Drain and rinse beans. Press Saute; heat oil in Instant Pot®. Add onions; cook and stir 5 to 7 minutes or until tender and lightly browned. Add garlic, tomato paste, oregano and salt; cook and stir 1 minute. Stir in beans, tomatoes and water; mix well.

2. Secure lid and move pressure release valve to Sealing position. Press Manual; cook at high pressure 16 minutes.

3. When cooking is complete, use natural release for 10 minutes, then release remaining pressure. Season with black pepper, if desired.

MAKES 8 TO 10 SERVINGS

WINTER SQUASH RISOTTO

2 tablespoons butter

1 tablespoon olive oil

1 large shallot or small onion, finely chopped

1½ cups uncooked arborio rice

1 teaspoon salt

½ teaspoon dried thyme

¼ teaspoon black pepper

¼ cup dry white wine

4 cups vegetable or chicken broth

2 cups cubed butternut squash (½-inch pieces)

½ grated Parmesan or Romano cheese, plus additional for garnish

1. Press Sauté; heat butter and oil in Instant Pot®. Add shallot; cook and stir 2 minutes or until softened. Add rice; cook and stir 4 minutes or until rice is translucent. Stir in salt, thyme and pepper. Add wine; cook and stir about 1 minute or until evaporated. Add broth and squash; mix well.

2. Secure lid and move pressure release valve to Sealing position. Press Manual; cook at high pressure 6 minutes.

3. When cooking is complete, press Cancel and use quick release.

4. Press Sauté; adjust heat to low ("less"). Cook risotto about 3 minutes or until desired consistency, stirring constantly. Stir in ½ cup cheese. Serve immediately with additional cheese.

MAKES 4 TO 6 SERVINGS

CHEESE GRITS WITH CHILES AND BACON

6 slices bacon, chopped

1 large shallot or small onion, finely chopped

1 serrano or jalapeño pepper, minced

3½ cups chicken broth

1 cup uncooked grits*

½ teaspoon salt

¼ teaspoon black pepper

1 cup (4 ounces) shredded Cheddar cheese

½ cup half-and-half

2 tablespoons finely chopped green onion

Do not use instant grits.

1. Press Sauté; cook bacon in Instant Pot® until crisp. Drain on paper towel-lined plate. Drain off all but 1 tablespoon drippings.

2. Add shallot and serrano pepper to pot; cook and stir 2 minutes or until shallot is lightly browned. Add broth, grits, salt and black pepper; cook and stir 1 minute.

3. Secure lid and move pressure release valve to Sealing position. Press Manual; cook at high pressure 14 minutes.

4. When cooking is complete, use natural release for 10 minutes, then release remaining pressure.

5. Stir grits until smooth. Add cheese, half-and-half and half of bacon; stir until well blended. Sprinkle with green onion and remaining bacon.

MAKES 4 SERVINGS

CLASSIC IRISH OATMEAL

2 tablespoons butter

1 cup steel-cut oats

3 cups water

½ teaspoon salt

½ teaspoon ground cinnamon

Berry Compote (recipe follows, optional)

⅓ cup half-and-half

¼ cup packed brown sugar

1. Press Sauté; melt butter in Instant Pot®. Add oats; cook about 6 minutes, stirring frequently. Add water, salt and cinnamon; cook and stir 1 minute.

2. Secure lid and move pressure release valve to Sealing position. Press Manual; cook at high pressure 13 minutes. Meanwhile, prepare Berry Compote, if desired.

3. When cooking is complete, press Cancel to turn off heat. Use natural release for 10 minutes, then release remaining pressure.

4. Stir oats until smooth. Add half-and-half and brown sugar; stir until well blended. If a thicker porridge is desired, press Sauté and cook 2 to 3 minutes or until desired thickness, stirring constantly. (Porridge will also thicken upon standing.) Serve with Berry Compote.

MAKES 4 SERVINGS

BERRY COMPOTE: Combine 1 cup quartered fresh strawberries, 6 ounces fresh blackberries, 6 ounces fresh blueberries, 3 tablespoons granulated sugar and 1 tablespoon water in medium saucepan; bring to a simmer over medium heat. Cook 8 to 9 minutes or until berries are tender but still hold their shape, stirring occasionally.

PESTO RICE AND BEANS

½ cup dried Great Northern beans, soaked 8 hours or overnight

1½ cups water or chicken broth, divided

¼ teaspoon salt, divided

½ cup uncooked long grain rice

4 ounces fresh green beans, cut into 1-inch pieces (about ¾ cup)

¼ cup prepared pesto

Shredded or grated Parmesan cheese, chopped plum tomatoes and chopped fresh parsley (optional)

1. Drain and rinse dried beans. Combine beans, 1 cup water and ⅛ teaspoon salt in Instant Pot®; mix well. Secure lid and move pressure release valve to Sealing position. Press Manual; cook at high pressure 4 minutes.

2. Meanwhile, rinse rice well; drain in fine-mesh strainer. Combine rice, remaining ½ cup water and ⅛ teaspoon salt in small metal or ceramic bowl that fits inside pot; mix well. Place green beans in center of 12-inch square of foil; sprinkle with additional salt. Bring up two sides of foil over beans; fold foil over several times to create packet. Fold in opposite ends. (Packet should measure about 8×4 inches.)

3. When cooking of beans is complete, press Cancel and use quick release. Place bowl with rice on rack; lower rack into pot. Arrange foil packet on top of bowl. (Packet should not entirely cover bowl.) Secure lid and move pressure release valve to Sealing position. Press Manual; cook at high pressure 4 minutes.

4. When cooking is complete, use natural release for 8 minutes, then release remaining pressure. Use handles of rack to remove bowl and foil packet from pot. If any liquid remains in bottom of pot with Great Northern beans, press Sauté; cook 1 to 2 minutes or until liquid is evaporated.

5. Add Great Northern beans and green beans to bowl with rice; gently stir in pesto. Top with cheese, tomatoes and parsley, if desired.

MAKES 4 SERVINGS

BLACK BEAN CHILI

1 pound dried black beans, soaked 8 hours or overnight

1 tablespoon olive oil

1 large onion, chopped

1 large jalapeño pepper, minced

3 cloves garlic, minced

2 tablespoons chili powder

2 teaspoons salt

1 teaspoon paprika

1 teaspoon dried oregano

1 teaspoon unsweetened cocoa powder

½ teaspoon ground cumin

¼ teaspoon ground cinnamon

2 cups water

1 can (about 14 ounces) diced tomatoes

1 bay leaf

1 to 2 tablespoons lime juice

Optional toppings: sour cream, picante sauce, sliced green onions, chopped fresh cilantro (optional)

1. Drain and rinse beans. Press Sauté; heat oil in Instant Pot®. Add onion; cook and stir 5 minutes. Add jalapeño, garlic, chili powder, salt, paprika, oregano, cocoa, cumin and cinnamon; cook and stir 1 minute. Add beans, water, tomatoes and bay leaf; mix well.

2. Secure lid and move pressure release valve to Sealing position. Press Manual; cook at high pressure 8 minutes.

3. When cooking is complete, use natural release for 15 minutes, then release remaining pressure.

4. For thicker chili, press Sauté; cook 3 to 5 minutes or until chili thickens, stirring frequently. (Chili will also thicken upon standing.) Remove and discard bay leaf. Stir in lime juice; serve with desired toppings.

MAKES 6 SERVINGS

TIP: For a heartier meal, hollow out small loaves of sourdough bread or crusty bread and serve the chili in bread bowls.

EASY DIRTY RICE

1½ cups uncooked long grain rice

8 ounces bulk Italian sausage

1½ cups water

1 onion, finely chopped

1 green bell pepper, finely chopped

½ cup finely chopped celery

1½ teaspoons salt

¼ teaspoon black pepper

¼ teaspoon ground red pepper

½ cup chopped fresh parsley

1. Rinse rice well; drain in fine-mesh strainer.

2. Press Sauté; cook sausage in Instant Pot® 6 to 8 minutes or until browned, stirring to break up meat. Drain fat. Stir in rice, water, onion, bell pepper, celery, salt, black pepper and red pepper; mix well.

3. Secure lid and move pressure release valve to Sealing position. Press Manual; cook at high pressure 4 minutes.

4. When cooking is complete, use natural release for 10 minutes, then release remaining pressure. Stir in parsley.

MAKES 4 TO 6 SERVINGS

BEAN AND PASTA SOUP

1¼ cups dried navy beans, soaked 8 hours or overnight

3 slices bacon, finely chopped

1 onion, chopped

1 stalk celery, chopped

1 carrot, chopped

2 cloves garlic, minced

4 cups water

1 smoked ham hock (8 to 12 ounces)

½ teaspoon salt

½ teaspoon dried thyme

½ teaspoon dried marjoram

¼ teaspoon black pepper

¾ cup uncooked small pasta shells

2 tablespoons chopped fresh parsley

½ to 1 cup chicken broth (optional)

Grated Parmesan cheese (optional)

1. Drain and rinse beans. Press Sauté; cook bacon in Instant Pot® until crisp. Add onion, celery and carrot; cook and stir 5 minutes or until golden brown, scraping up browned bits from bottom of pot. Add garlic; cook and stir 30 seconds. Add beans, water, ham hock, salt, thyme, marjoram and pepper; mix well.

2. Secure lid and move pressure release valve to Sealing position. Press Manual; cook at high pressure 16 minutes.

3. When cooking is complete, use natural release for 10 minutes, then release remaining pressure.

4. Remove ham hock to plate. Use immersion blender to partially purée soup, leaving soup chunky. (Or remove half of soup to food processor or blender; process until smooth and return puréed soup to pot.)

5. Press Sauté; bring soup to a boil. Stir in pasta. Adjust heat to low ("less"); cook about 10 minutes or until pasta is tender, stirring occasionally.

6. Meanwhile, remove meat from ham hock; chop into bite-size pieces. Stir meat and parsley into soup. If necessary, thin soup with broth. Garnish with cheese.

MAKES 4 SERVINGS

FOUR-BEAN CHILI STEW

¾ cup dried kidney beans

¾ cup dried chickpeas

¾ cup dried Great Northern beans

¾ cup dried black beans

2 cans (about 11 ounces each) tomatillos, drained

1 can (about 15 ounces) tomato sauce

1½ cups water

1 cup prepared barbecue sauce

1 onion, chopped

3 cloves garlic, minced

1½ teaspoons ground cumin

1½ teaspoons chili powder

½ teaspoon salt

¼ teaspoon ground red pepper

1 zucchini, cut in half then cut into 1-inch slices

½ red bell pepper, chopped

Flour tortillas, warmed (optional)

Optional toppings: sour cream, chopped tomato, chopped onion, shredded Cheddar cheese, chopped fresh cilantro (optional)

1. Rinse beans separately in colander under cold water, picking out any debris or blemished beans. Combine kidney beans, chickpeas and Great Northern beans in large bowl; cover with water. Place black beans in medium bowl; cover with water.* Soak 8 hours or overnight.

2. Drain and rinse all beans. Place in Instant Pot® with tomatillos, tomato sauce, 1½ cups water, barbecue sauce, onion, garlic, cumin, chili powder, salt and ground red pepper; mix well.

3. Secure lid and move pressure release valve to Sealing position. Press Manual; cook at high pressure 20 minutes.

4. When cooking is complete, use natural release for 5 minutes, then release remaining pressure.

5. Stir in zucchini and bell pepper. Secure lid and move pressure release valve to Sealing position. Press Manual; cook at high pressure 1 minute. When cooking is complete, press Cancel and use quick release. Serve with tortillas and desired garnishes.

Soaking black beans with the other beans will turn the Great Northerns and chickpeas purple.

MAKES 6 SERVINGS

1¾ cups uncooked long grain rice

2 tablespoons butter

1¾ cups vegetable or chicken broth

1 teaspoon Greek seasoning

1 teaspoon dried oregano

¼ teaspoon salt

1 cup pitted kalamata olives, drained and chopped

¾ cup chopped roasted red peppers

Crumbled feta cheese (optional)

Chopped fresh Italian parsley (optional)

1. Rinse rice well; drain in fine-mesh strainer.

2. Press Sauté; melt butter in Instant Pot®. Add rice; cook 5 to 6 minutes or until golden brown, stirring occasionally. Add broth, Greek seasoning, oregano and salt; mix well.

3. Secure lid and move pressure release valve to Sealing position. Press Manual; cook at high pressure 4 minutes.

4. When cooking is complete, use natural release for 10 minutes, then release remaining pressure.

5. Stir in olives and roasted red peppers; garnish with cheese and parsley.

MAKES 6 TO 8 SERVINGS

SUPERFOOD BREAKFAST PORRIDGE

¾ cup steel-cut oats

¼ cup uncooked quinoa, rinsed and drained

¼ cup dried cranberries, plus additional for serving

¼ cup raisins

3 tablespoons ground flax seeds

2 tablespoons chia seeds

1 teaspoon olive oil

¼ teaspoon salt

¼ teaspoon ground cinnamon

2½ cups almond milk, plus additional for serving

1½ cups water

Maple syrup (optional)

¼ cup sliced almonds, toasted* (optional)

To toast almonds, cook and stir in small skillet over medium heat 1 to 2 minutes or until lightly browned.

1. Spray heatproof bowl (metal, glass or ceramic) that fits inside of Instant Pot® with nonstick cooking spray. Combine oats, quinoa, ¼ cup cranberries, raisins, flax seeds, chia seeds, oil, salt and cinnamon in prepared bowl; mix well. Stir in 2½ cups almond milk until blended.

2. Pour water into pot. Place rack in pot; place bowl on rack. Secure lid and move pressure release valve to Sealing position. Press Manual; cook at high pressure 13 minutes.

3. When cooking is complete, use natural release.

4. Stir porridge until smooth. Serve with additional almond milk, cranberries, maple syrup and almonds, if desired.

MAKES 4 SERVINGS

QUINOA AND MANGO SALAD

1 cup uncooked quinoa

1½ cups water

¾ teaspoon salt, divided

2 cups cubed peeled mango (about 2 large mangoes)

½ cup sliced green onions

½ cup dried cranberries

2 tablespoons chopped fresh parsley

¼ cup extra virgin olive oil

1½ tablespoons white wine vinegar

1 teaspoon Dijon mustard

⅛ teaspoon black pepper

1. Place quinoa in fine-mesh strainer; rinse under cold running water and drain. Combine quinoa, 1½ cups water and ¼ teaspoon salt in Instant Pot®; mix well.

2. Secure lid and move pressure release valve to Sealing position. Press Manual; cook at high pressure 1 minute.

3. When cooking is complete, use natural release for 10 minutes, then release remaining pressure.

4. Press Sauté; cook and stir 1 minute or until any excess water has evaporated. Spread quinoa on large plate or in baking dish; cover loosely and refrigerate at least 1 hour.

5. Add mangoes, green onions, cranberries and parsley to quinoa; mix well. Combine oil, vinegar, mustard, remaining ½ teaspoon salt and pepper in small bowl; whisk until blended. Pour over quinoa mixture; stir until well blended.

MAKES 6 SERVINGS

TIP: This salad can be made several hours ahead and refrigerated. Let stand at room temperature for at least 30 minutes before serving.

HEARTY WHITE BEAN SOUP

1½ cups dried navy beans,
  soaked 8 hours or
  overnight

2 tablespoons olive oil

1 cup chopped onion

1 cup chopped carrots

1 cup chopped red or
  green bell pepper

½ cup chopped celery

2 cloves garlic, minced

1 tablespoon chopped fresh
  oregano *or* 1 teaspoon
  dried oregano

1½ teaspoons chopped fresh
  thyme *or* ¾ teaspoon
  dried thyme

½ teaspoon ground cumin

4 cups vegetable or chicken
  broth

3 cups water

2 teaspoons salt

¼ teaspoon black pepper

1. Drain and rinse beans. Press Sauté; heat oil in Instant Pot®. Add onion; cook and stir 3 minutes or until softened. Add carrots, bell pepper and celery; cook and stir 3 minutes. Add garlic, oregano, thyme and cumin; cook and stir 1 minute. Stir in beans, broth, water, salt and black pepper; mix well.

2. Secure lid and move pressure release valve to Sealing position. Press Manual; cook at high pressure 15 minutes.

3. When cooking is complete, use natural release.

MAKES 6 SERVINGS

MINESTRONE ALLA MILANESE

¾ cup dried cannellini beans, soaked 8 hours or overnight

2 tablespoons olive oil

1 cup chopped carrots (½-inch pieces)

1 stalk celery, halved lengthwise and cut crosswise into ¼-inch slices

¾ cup chopped onion

2 cloves garlic, minced

1 container (32 ounces) vegetable broth

1 can (about 14 ounces) diced tomatoes

1 cup diced unpeeled red potato (about 1 large)

1 cup coarsely chopped green cabbage

1 small zucchini, halved lengthwise and cut crosswise into ¼-inch slices

¾ cup sliced fresh green beans

1½ teaspoons salt

½ teaspoon dried basil

¼ teaspoon dried rosemary

¼ teaspoon black pepper

1 bay leaf

Shredded Parmesan cheese (optional)

1. Drain and rinse dried beans. Press Sauté; heat oil in Instant Pot®. Add carrots, celery and onion; cook and stir 5 minutes or until vegetables are softened. Add garlic; cook and stir 1 minute. Stir in broth, tomatoes, potato, cabbage, zucchini, green beans, salt, basil, rosemary, pepper and bay leaf; mix well.

2. Secure lid and move pressure release valve to Sealing position. Press Manual; cook at high pressure 10 minutes.

3. When cooking is complete, use natural release for 15 minutes, then release remaining pressure. Remove and discard bay leaf. Garnish with cheese.

MAKES 6 SERVINGS

FARRO RISOTTO WITH MUSHROOMS AND SPINACH

2 tablespoons olive oil, divided

1 onion, chopped

12 ounces cremini mushrooms, stems trimmed and quartered

1 teaspoon salt

¼ teaspoon black pepper

2 cloves garlic, minced

1 cup uncooked pearled farro

1 sprig fresh thyme

1½ cups vegetable or chicken broth

1 package (5 to 6 ounces) baby spinach

½ cup grated Parmesan cheese

1. Press Sauté; heat 1 tablespoon oil in Instant Pot®. Add onion; cook and stir 5 minutes or until translucent. Add remaining 1 tablespoon oil, mushrooms, salt and pepper; cook about 8 minutes or until mushrooms have released their liquid and are browned, stirring occasionally. Add garlic; cook and stir 1 minute. Add farro and thyme; cook and stir 1 minute. Add broth; mix well.

2. Secure lid and move pressure release valve to Sealing position. Press Manual; cook at high pressure 10 minutes.

3. When cooking is complete, use natural release for 10 minutes, then release remaining pressure. Remove and discard thyme sprig.

4. Stir in spinach and cheese until spinach is wilted.

MAKES 4 SERVINGS

SPLIT PEA SOUP

8 slices bacon, chopped

1 onion, chopped

2 carrots, chopped

1 stalk celery, chopped

1 clove garlic, minced

½ teaspoon dried thyme

1 container (32 ounces) chicken broth

2 cups water

1 package (16 ounces) dried split peas, rinsed and sorted

¾ teaspoon salt

½ teaspoon black pepper

1 bay leaf

1. Press Sauté; cook and stir bacon in Instant Pot® until crisp. Remove to paper towel-lined plate. Drain off all but 1 tablespoon drippings.

2. Add onion, carrots and celery to pot; cook and stir 5 minutes or until vegetables are softened. Add garlic and thyme; cook and stir 1 minute. Stir in broth and water, scraping up browned bits from bottom of pot. Add split peas, half of bacon, salt, pepper and bay leaf; mix well.

3. Secure lid and move pressure release valve to Sealing position. Press Manual; cook at high pressure 8 minutes.

4. When cooking is complete, use natural release for 10 minutes, then release remaining pressure. Stir soup; remove and discard bay leaf. Garnish with remaining bacon.

MAKES 4 TO 6 SERVINGS

NOTE: The soup may seem thin immediately after cooking, but it will thicken upon standing. If prepared in advance and refrigerated, thin the soup with water when reheating until it reaches the desired consistency.

CHANNA CHAT (INDIAN-SPICED SNACK MIX)

1 cup dried chickpeas, soaked 8 hours or overnight

2 teaspoons canola oil

1 medium onion, finely chopped, divided

2 cloves garlic, minced

2 cups vegetable broth or water

1 tablespoon tomato paste

1 teaspoon salt

½ teaspoon ground cinnamon

½ teaspoon ground cumin

¼ teaspoon black pepper

1 bay leaf

½ cup balsamic vinegar

1 tablespoon packed brown sugar

1 plum tomato, chopped

½ jalapeño pepper, minced or ¼ teaspoon ground red pepper (optional)

½ cup crisp rice cereal

3 tablespoons chopped fresh cilantro (optional)

1. Drain and rinse beans. Press Sauté; heat oil in Instant Pot®. Add half of onion and garlic; cook and stir 2 minutes or until softened. Stir in chickpeas, broth, tomato paste, salt, cinnamon, cumin, black pepper and bay leaf; mix well.

2. Secure lid and move pressure release valve to Sealing position. Press Manual; cook at high pressure 15 minutes.

3. When cooking is complete, use natural release for 10 minutes, then release remaining pressure. Remove lid; let chickpeas cool in liquid 15 minutes.

4. Meanwhile, combine balsamic vinegar and brown sugar in small saucepan; cook over medium-low heat 5 minutes or until mixture reduces and becomes syrupy.

5. Drain off and discard 1 cup liquid from chickpeas; remove and discard bay leaf. Toss chickpeas with tomato, remaining onion and jalapeño, if desired. Fold in rice cereal; drizzle with balsamic syrup. Garnish with cilantro.

MAKES 6 TO 8 SERVINGS

MUSHROOM BARLEY SOUP

2 tablespoons olive oil

1 onion, chopped

2 carrots, chopped

2 stalks celery, chopped

3 cloves garlic, minced

1 teaspoon salt

½ teaspoon dried thyme

½ teaspoon black pepper

5 cups vegetable or chicken broth

1 package (16 ounces) sliced mushrooms

½ cup uncooked pearled barley

½ ounce dried porcini or shiitake mushrooms

1. Press Sauté; heat oil in Instant Pot®. Add onion, carrots and celery; cook and stir 5 minutes or until vegetables are softened. Add garlic, salt, thyme and pepper; cook and stir 1 minute. Stir in broth, sliced mushrooms, barley and dried mushrooms; mix well.

2. Secure lid and move pressure release valve to Sealing position. Press Manual; cook at high pressure 22 minutes.

3. When cooking is complete, use natural release for 10 minutes, then release remaining pressure.

MAKES 6 TO 8 SERVINGS

BBQ "BAKED" BEANS

1 package (16 ounces) dried Great Northern beans, soaked 8 hours or overnight

4 slices bacon, chopped

1 onion, chopped

2 cloves garlic, minced

1 can (about 14 ounces) diced tomatoes

1 cup water

¼ cup ketchup

3 tablespoons maple syrup

3 tablespoons molasses

2 tablespoons packed brown sugar

¾ teaspoon salt

½ teaspoon dry mustard

⅛ teaspoon black pepper

1. Drain and rinse beans. Press Sauté; cook bacon in Instant Pot® until crisp.

2. Add onion; cook and stir 3 minutes or until softened. Add garlic; cook and stir 1 minute. Stir in beans, tomatoes, water, ketchup, maple syrup, molasses, brown sugar, salt, mustard and pepper; mix well.

3. Secure lid and move pressure release valve to Sealing position. Press Manual; cook at high pressure 45 minutes.

4. When cooking is complete, use natural release for 10 minutes, then release remaining pressure.

MAKES 4 TO 6 SERVINGS

VARIATION: For a vegetarian version, omit the bacon. Sauté the onion and garlic in 1 tablespoon olive oil in step 1, then proceed as directed above.

CREAMY BARLEY RISOTTO

1 tablespoon olive oil

1 large leek, halved and thinly sliced

1 cup uncooked pearled barley

1 teaspoon salt

2 cups vegetable broth

¼ teaspoon black pepper

1 cup frozen peas

½ cup shredded Parmesan cheese

2 tablespoons butter, cut into pieces

1 tablespoon lemon juice

1 teaspoon grated lemon peel, plus additional for garnish

Shaved Parmesan cheese (optional)

Chopped fresh Italian parsley (optional)

1. Press Sauté; heat oil in Instant Pot®. Add leek; cook and stir 3 minutes or until softened and beginning to lightly brown. Add barley and salt; cook and stir 1 minute. Stir in broth and pepper; mix well.

2. Secure lid and move pressure release valve to Sealing position. Press Manual; cook at high pressure 18 minutes.

3. When cooking is complete, use natural release for 10 minutes, then release remaining pressure.

4. Stir in peas, ½ cup cheese, butter, lemon juice and 1 teaspoon lemon peel. Garnish with additional cheese, lemon peel and parsley.

MAKES 4 SERVINGS

MIDDLE EASTERN LENTIL SOUP

2 tablespoons olive oil

1 small onion, chopped

1 medium red bell pepper, chopped

1 teaspoon whole fennel seeds

½ teaspoon ground cumin

¼ teaspoon ground red pepper

4 cups water

1 cup dried lentils, rinsed and sorted

1½ teaspoons salt

1 tablespoon lemon juice

½ cup plain yogurt

2 tablespoons chopped fresh parsley

1. Press Sauté; heat oil in Instant Pot®. Add onion and bell pepper; cook and stir 3 minutes or until vegetables are softened. Add fennel seeds, cumin and ground red pepper; cook and stir 1 minute. Stir in water, lentils and salt; mix well.

2. Secure lid and move pressure release valve to Sealing position. Press Manual; cook at high pressure 17 minutes.

3. When cooking is complete, use natural release for 10 minutes, then release remaining pressure.

4. Stir in lemon juice. Top soup with yogurt; sprinkle with parsley.

MAKES 4 SERVINGS

SERVING SUGGESTION: Serve with homemade pita chips. Cut 4 pita bread rounds into 6 wedges each. Spread pita wedges on large baking sheet. Brush with 1 tablespoon olive oil; sprinkle with 1 teaspoon coarse salt. Bake at 350°F 15 minutes or until lightly browned and crisp.

PAELLA SALAD

1 cup uncooked brown rice

1 cup chicken broth

¼ teaspoon salt

¼ teaspoon ground turmeric

1 jar (6 ounces) marinated artichokes, drained and marinade liquid reserved

1 tablespoon minced onion

¼ teaspoon dried oregano

1 cup small peeled cooked shrimp (with tails on)

½ cup thawed frozen peas

2 ounces pepperoni, cut into thin julienne strips

1 jar (2 ounces) diced pimientos, drained

Black pepper

1. Rinse rice well; drain in fine-mesh strainer. Combine rice, broth, ¼ teaspoon salt and turmeric in Instant Pot®; mix well.

2. Secure lid and move pressure release valve to Sealing position. Press Manual; cook at high pressure 22 minutes.

3. When cooking is complete, use natural release for 10 minutes, then release remaining pressure.

4. Transfer rice to large bowl; stir in reserved artichoke marinade, onion and oregano. Fluff rice with fork. Refrigerate 20 minutes or until cool.

5. Add artichokes, shrimp, peas, pepperoni and pimientos to rice mixture; stir gently until blended. Season with additional salt and pepper.

MAKES 4 SERVINGS

ASIAN KALE AND CHICKPEAS

2 cups dried chickpeas, soaked 8 hours or overnight

1 tablespoon plus 1 teaspoon sesame oil, divided

1 medium onion, thinly sliced

2 teaspoons grated fresh ginger, divided

2 cloves garlic, minced, divided

2 jalapeño peppers, finely chopped, divided

2 cups vegetable broth

½ cup water

1 teaspoon salt

8 cups loosely packed chopped kale (about 1 bunch)

1 tablespoon lime juice

1 teaspoon grated lime peel

Hot cooked rice

1. Drain and rinse chickpeas. Press Sauté; heat 1 tablespoon oil in Instant Pot®. Add onion, 1 teaspoon ginger, 1 clove garlic and 1 jalapeño; cook and stir 3 minutes or until onion is softened. Stir in chickpeas, broth, water and salt; mix well.

2. Secure lid and move pressure release valve to Sealing position. Press Manual; cook at high pressure 15 minutes.

3. When cooking is complete, use natural release for 10 minutes, then release remaining pressure. Stir in kale. Secure lid and move pressure release valve to Sealing position. Cook at high pressure 3 minutes.

4. When cooking is complete, press Cancel and use quick release.

5. If there is excess liquid in pot, press Sauté and cook 2 to 3 minutes or until liquid evaporates. Stir in remaining 1 teaspoon oil, 1 teaspoon ginger, 1 clove garlic, 1 jalapeño, lime juice and lime peel. Season with additional salt, if desired. Serve with rice, if desired.

MAKES 4 TO 6 SERVINGS

ASPARAGUS-PARMESAN RISOTTO

4 tablespoons butter, divided

1 tablespoon olive oil

1 onion, finely chopped

1½ cups uncooked arborio rice

1 teaspoon salt

¼ cup dry white wine

4 cups vegetable broth

2½ cups fresh asparagus pieces (about 1 inch)

⅔ cup frozen peas

1 cup grated Parmesan cheese

Shaved Parmesan cheese (optional)

1. Press Sauté; heat 3 tablespoons butter and oil in Instant Pot®. Add onion; cook and stir 2 minutes or until softened. Add rice; cook and stir 2 minutes or until rice is translucent. Stir in salt. Add wine; cook and stir about 1 minute or until evaporated. Add broth; mix well.

2. Secure lid and move pressure release valve to Sealing position. Press Manual; cook at high pressure 5 minutes.

3. When cooking is complete, press Cancel and use quick release. Stir in asparagus and peas. Secure lid and move pressure release valve to Sealing position. Cook at high pressure 1 minute.

4. When cooking is complete, press Cancel and use quick release. Stir in remaining 1 tablespoon butter and 1 cup cheese. Serve immediately; garnish with additional cheese, if desired.

MAKES 4 TO 6 SERVINGS

BARLEY WITH CURRANTS AND PINE NUTS

2 tablespoons butter

1 onion, finely chopped

2 cups vegetable broth

1 cup uncooked pearled barley

½ cup currants

½ teaspoon salt

¼ teaspoon black pepper

2 ounces (about ½ cup) pine nuts, toasted*

To toast pine nuts, cook in small skillet over medium heat 2 minutes or until lightly browned, stirring frequently.

1. Press Sauté; melt butter in Instant Pot®. Add onion; cook and stir 5 minutes or until tender. Stir in broth, barley, currants, salt and pepper; mix well.

2. Secure lid and move pressure release valve to Sealing position. Press Manual; cook at high pressure 18 minutes.

3. When cooking is complete, use natural release for 10 minutes, then release remaining pressure.

4. Stir in pine nuts. Serve warm or at room temperature.

MAKES 4 TO 6 SERVINGS

BULGUR PILAF WITH CARAMELIZED ONIONS AND KALE

1 tablespoon olive oil

1 small onion, cut into thin wedges

1 clove garlic, minced

2 cups chopped kale

2¾ cups vegetable or chicken broth

1 cup medium grain bulgur

1 teaspoon salt

¼ teaspoon black pepper

1. Press Sauté; heat oil in Instant Pot®. Add onion; cook about 10 minutes or until golden brown, stirring frequently. Add garlic; cook and stir 1 minute. Add kale; cook and stir about 1 minute or until wilted. Stir in broth, bulgur, salt and pepper; mix well.

2. Secure lid and move pressure release valve to Sealing position. Press Manual; cook at high pressure 8 minutes.

3. When cooking is complete, use natural release for 5 minutes, then release remaining pressure.

MAKES 4 SERVINGS

PUMPKIN RISOTTO

2 tablespoons butter

1 tablespoon olive oil

1 onion, finely chopped

2 cloves garlic, minced

1½ cups uncooked arborio rice

1 teaspoon salt

¼ teaspoon ground nutmeg

⅛ teaspoon black pepper

½ cup dry white wine

4 cups vegetable broth

1 can (15 ounces) solid-pack pumpkin

5 fresh sage leaves

½ cup shredded Parmesan cheese, plus additional for serving

¼ cup roasted pumpkin seeds (pepitas)

1. Press Sauté; heat butter and oil in Instant Pot®. Add onion and garlic; cook and stir 3 minutes or until softened. Add rice; cook and stir 4 minutes or until rice is translucent. Stir in salt, nutmeg and pepper. Add wine; cook and stir about 1 minute or until evaporated. Stir in broth, pumpkin and sage; mix well.

2. Secure lid and move pressure release valve to Sealing position. Press Manual; cook at high pressure 6 minutes.

3. When cooking is complete, press Cancel and use quick release.

4. Press Sauté; adjust heat to low ("less"). Cook about 3 minutes or risotto reaches desired consistency, stirring constantly. Stir in ½ cup cheese until blended. Serve immediately with additional cheese and pepitas.

MAKES 4 SERVINGS

MUSHROOM AND CHICKPEA RAGOÛT

1 cup dried chickpeas, soaked 8 hours or overnight

3 tablespoons olive oil

8 ounces sliced cremini mushrooms

8 ounces shiitake mushrooms,* stemmed and thinly sliced

1 onion, chopped

4 cloves garlic, minced

½ cup Madeira wine

2 teaspoons salt

1 teaspoon dried rosemary

Black pepper

1 can (28 ounces) crushed tomatoes

1 cup water

1 can (6 ounces) tomato paste

Polenta (recipe follows)

*Or substitute an additional 8 ounces of cremini mushrooms for the shiitake mushrooms.

1. Drain and rinse chickpeas. Press Sauté; heat oil in Instant Pot®. Add mushrooms, onion and garlic; cook and stir 6 minutes or until mushrooms are browned. Add Madeira, salt and rosemary; cook and stir 1 to 2 minutes or until liquid is almost evaporated. Season with pepper. Stir in tomatoes, water, chickpeas and tomato paste; mix well.

2. Secure lid and move pressure release valve to Sealing position. Press Manual; cook at high pressure 22 minutes.

3. When cooking is complete, use natural release for 10 minutes, then release remaining pressure. Meanwhile, prepare Polenta.

4. When cooking is complete, use natural release for 10 minutes, then release remaining pressure. Serve over Polenta.

MAKES 6 SERVINGS

POLENTA: Combine 2 cups milk, 2 cups water and ¼ teaspoon salt in large saucepan; bring to a boil over medium-high heat. Slowly whisk in 1 cup instant polenta in thin steady stream. Cook 4 to 5 minutes or until thick and creamy, whisking constantly. Remove from heat; stir in ½ cup grated Parmesan cheese.

CHICKEN CONGEE

4 cups water

4 cups chicken broth

2 chicken leg quarters *or* 4 chicken drumsticks, skin removed (1 to 1½ pounds)

1 cup white jasmine rice, rinsed well and drained

1 (1-inch) piece ginger, cut into ¼-inch slices

1 teaspoon salt

½ teaspoon white pepper

Optional toppings: soy sauce, sesame oil, sliced green onions, shredded carrot, salted roasted peanuts and/or pickled vegetables

1. Combine water, broth, chicken, rice, ginger, salt and pepper in Instant Pot®; mix well.

2. Secure lid and move pressure release valve to Sealing position. Press Manual; cook at high pressure 20 minutes.

3. When cooking is complete, use natural release for 15 minutes, then release remaining pressure. Remove and discard ginger. Remove chicken to plate; set aside until cool enough to handle.

4. Meanwhile, press Sauté; cook and stir congee 2 to 3 minutes or until desired consistency is reached. Shred chicken; stir into congee. Serve with desired toppings.

MAKES 6 SERVINGS

BARLEY AND VEGETABLE RISOTTO

1 tablespoon olive oil

1 onion, chopped

1 cup uncooked pearled barley

2 cloves garlic, minced

1½ cups vegetable broth

8 ounces sliced mushrooms

1 large red bell pepper, diced

1 teaspoon salt

2 cups packed baby spinach

½ cup grated Parmesan cheese

¼ teaspoon black pepper

1. Press Sauté; heat oil in Instant Pot®. Add onion; cook and stir 3 minutes or until softened. Add barley and garlic; cook and stir 1 minute. Stir in broth, mushrooms, bell pepper and salt; mix well.

2. Secure lid and move pressure release valve to Sealing position. Press Manual; cook at high pressure 18 minutes.

3. When cooking is complete, use natural release for 10 minutes, then release remaining pressure.

4. Stir in spinach; let stand 2 to 3 minutes or until spinach is wilted. Gently stir in cheese and black pepper.

MAKES 4 TO 6 SERVINGS

VEGETARIAN CHILI

2 tablespoons olive oil

1 onion, finely chopped

2 medium carrots, chopped

1 red bell pepper, chopped

3 tablespoons chili powder

2 tablespoons tomato paste

2 tablespoons packed dark
    brown sugar

2 tablespoons ground
    cumin

3 cloves garlic, minced

1 tablespoon dried oregano

2 teaspoons salt

1 can (28 ounces) diced
    tomatoes

1 can (about 15 ounces)
    tomato sauce

1 can (about 15 ounces)
    small white beans,
    rinsed and drained

1 can (about 15 ounces)
    light kidney beans,
    rinsed and drained

1 can (about 15 ounces)
    dark kidney beans,
    rinsed and drained

1 can (about 15 ounces)
    pinto beans, rinsed
    and drained

1 can (4 ounces) diced
    mild green chiles

1 ounce unsweetened
    chocolate, chopped

1 tablespoon cider vinegar

1. Press Sauté; heat oil in Instant Pot®. Add onion, carrots and bell pepper; cook and stir 5 minutes or until vegetables are softened. Add chili powder, tomato paste, brown sugar, cumin, garlic, oregano and salt; cook and stir 1 minute. Stir in tomatoes, tomato sauce, beans and chiles; mix well.

2. Secure lid and move pressure release valve to Sealing position. Press Manual; cook at high pressure 10 minutes.

3. When cooking is complete, use natural release for 10 minutes, then release remaining pressure. Stir in chocolate and vinegar until blended.

MAKES 8 TO 10 SERVINGS

SPINACH RISOTTO

2 tablespoons olive oil

2 tablespoons butter, divided

1 shallot, finely chopped

1½ cups uncooked arborio rice

1½ teaspoons salt

¼ teaspoon black pepper

½ cup dry white wine

4 cups vegetable broth

2 cups packed baby spinach

½ cup shredded Parmesan cheese,

2 tablespoons pine nuts, toasted*

*To toast pine nuts, cook in small skillet over medium heat 2 minutes or until lightly browned, stirring frequently.

1. Press Sauté; heat oil and 1 tablespoon butter in Instant Pot®. Add shallot; cook and stir 2 minutes or until softened. Add rice; cook and stir 3 minutes or until rice is translucent. Stir in salt and pepper. Add wine; cook and stir about 1 minute or until evaporated. Stir in broth; mix well.

2. Secure lid and move pressure release valve to Sealing position. Press Manual; cook at high pressure 6 minutes.

3. When cooking is complete, press Cancel and use quick release.

4. Press Sauté; adjust heat to low ("less"). Add spinach to pot; cook about 3 minutes or until spinach is wilted and risotto reaches desired consistency, stirring constantly. Stir in cheese and remaining 1 tablespoon butter until blended. Sprinkle with pine nuts.

MAKES 4 SERVINGS

LENTIL RICE SOUP

1 tablespoon olive oil

1 onion, finely chopped

2 carrots, finely chopped

2 stalks celery, finely chopped

2 teaspoons minced garlic

1 teaspoon salt

1 teaspoon herbes de Provence

⅛ teaspoon black pepper

6 cups vegetable broth

1 cup dried lentils, rinsed and sorted

¼ cup uncooked rice, rinsed well

¼ cup chopped fresh parsley

Sour cream (optional)

1. Press Sauté; heat oil in Instant Pot®. Add onion, carrots, celery and garlic; cook and stir 5 minutes or until vegetables are softened. Add salt, herbes de Provence and pepper; cook and stir 30 seconds. Stir in broth, lentils and rice; mix well.

2. Secure lid and move pressure release valve to Sealing position. Press Manual; cook at high pressure 10 minutes.

3. When cooking is complete, use natural release for 10 minutes, then release remaining pressure. Stir in parsley. Serve with sour cream, if desired.

MAKES 4 TO 6 SERVINGS

FRIJOLES BORRACHOS (DRUNKEN BEANS)

1 pound dried pinto
   beans, soaked
   8 hours or
   overnight

6 slices bacon,
   chopped

1 large onion,
   chopped

3 jalapeño peppers,
   seeded and
   finely chopped

1 tablespoon minced
   garlic

1 tablespoon dried
   oregano

1 cup dark
   Mexican beer

1 can (about
   14 ounces) diced
   tomatoes

1 cup water

¾ teaspoon salt

¼ cup chopped
   fresh cilantro

1. Drain and rinse beans. Press Sauté; cook bacon in
   Instant Pot® until crisp. Drain off all but 2 tablespoons
   drippings. Add onion to pot; cook and stir 3 minutes
   or until softened and lightly browned. Add jalapeños,
   garlic and oregano; cook and stir 1 minute. Stir in beer,
   scraping up browned bits from bottom of pot. Stir in
   beans, tomatoes, water and salt; mix well.

2. Secure lid and move pressure release valve to Sealing
   position. Press Manual; cook at high pressure 22 minutes.

3. When cooking is complete, use natural release for
   10 minutes, then release remaining pressure.

4. Press Sauté; cook 3 minutes, mashing beans slightly
   until broth is thickened and creamy. Stir in cilantro.

MAKES 6 TO 8 SERVINGS

QUICK CHICKEN AND BEAN STEW

1 pound boneless skinless chicken thighs, cut into 1-inch pieces

1 can (about 15 ounces) Great Northern beans, rinsed and drained

1 can (about 15 ounces) black beans, rinsed and drained

1 can (about 14 ounces) crushed tomatoes (preferably fire-roasted)

1 onion, chopped

⅓ cup chicken broth

Juice of 1 large orange (about ⅓ cup)

1 canned chipotle pepper in adobo sauce, minced

1 teaspoon salt

1 teaspoon ground cumin

1 bay leaf

Fresh cilantro sprigs (optional)

1. Combine chicken, beans, tomatoes, onion, broth, orange juice, chipotle pepper, salt, cumin and bay leaf in Instant Pot®; mix well.

2. Secure lid and move pressure release valve to Sealing position. Press Manual; cook at high pressure 6 minutes.

3. When cooking is complete, use natural release for 5 minutes, then release remaining pressure.

4. Press Sauté; cook 3 to 5 minutes or until stew thickens slightly, stirring frequently. Remove and discard bay leaf. Garnish with cilantro.

MAKES 4 TO 6 SERVINGS

APPLE-CINNAMON BREAKFAST RISOTTO

4 tablespoons
(½ stick) butter

4 medium Granny
Smith apples
(about 1½ pounds),
peeled and diced

1½ teaspoons ground
cinnamon, divided

1½ cups uncooked
arborio rice

1 teaspoon salt

¼ teaspoon ground
allspice

4 cups apple juice

2 tablespoons packed
dark brown sugar,
plus additional
for serving

1 teaspoon vanilla

Milk, sliced
almonds and
dried cranberries
(optional)

1. Press Sauté; melt 2 tablespoons butter in Instant Pot®. Add apples and ½ teaspoon cinnamon; cook and stir about 5 minutes or until apples are softened. Transfer apples to small bowl; set aside.

2. Melt remaining 2 tablespoons butter in pot. Add rice, remaining 1 teaspoon cinnamon, salt and allspice; cook and stir 1 minute. Stir in apple juice, 2 tablespoons brown sugar and vanilla; mix well.

3. Secure lid and move pressure release valve to Sealing position. Press Manual; cook at high pressure 6 minutes.

4. When cooking is complete, press Cancel and use quick release.

5. Press Sauté; add reserved apples to pot. Cook and stir 1 minute or until risotto reaches desired consistency. Serve with milk, almonds, cranberries and additional brown sugar, if desired.

MAKES 6 SERVINGS

SOUTHWESTERN MAC AND CHEESE

4 tablespoons (½ stick) butter, divided

1 onion, finely chopped

3⅓ cups water

1 package (16 ounces) uncooked elbow macaroni

1 can (about 14 ounces) diced tomatoes with green peppers and onions

1 teaspoon salt

4 cups (16 ounces) shredded Mexican cheese blend, divided

½ cup milk

1 cup salsa

1. Press Sauté; melt 1 tablespoon butter in Instant Pot®. Add onion; cook and stir 3 minutes or until softened. Stir in water, macaroni, tomatoes and salt; mix well.

2. Secure lid and move pressure release valve to Sealing position. Press Manual; cook at high pressure 4 minutes.

3. When cooking is complete, press Cancel and use quick release.

4. Press Sauté; add 3½ cups cheese, milk and remaining 3 tablespoons butter to pot. Stir until smooth and well blended. Stir in salsa. Press Cancel. Sprinkle remaining ½ cup cheese over pasta; let stand until melted.

MAKES 6 TO 8 SERVINGS

MUSHROOM RISOTTO

2 tablespoons olive oil

¾ cup chopped shallots *or* 1 small onion, chopped

8 ounces sliced mushrooms

3 cloves garlic, minced

1½ cups arborio rice

¼ cup Madeira wine

3½ cups vegetable broth

½ teaspoon salt

¼ teaspoon black pepper

⅔ cup grated Romano cheese

3 tablespoons chopped fresh parsley

2 tablespoons butter

1. Press Sauté; heat oil in Instant Pot®. Add shallots; cook and stir 2 minutes or until softened. Add mushrooms; cook and stir about 6 minutes or until liquid evaporates and mushrooms begin to brown. Add garlic; cook and stir 30 seconds. Add rice; cook and stir 1 minute. Add Madeira; cook and stir 1 minute or until almost evaporated. Stir in broth, salt and pepper; mix well.

2. Secure lid and move pressure release valve to Sealing or locked position. Press Manual; cook at high pressure 6 minutes.

3. When cooking is complete, press Cancel and use quick release.

4. Press Sauté; adjust heat to low ("less"). Cook about 3 minutes or until risotto reaches desired consistency, stirring constantly. Stir in cheese, parsley and butter until blended.

MAKES 4 SERVINGS

CHEESY POLENTA

5 cups vegetable or chicken broth

½ teaspoon salt

1½ cups uncooked instant polenta

½ cup grated Parmesan cheese, plus additional for serving

4 tablespoons (½ stick) butter, cubed

Fried sage leaves (optional)

1. Combine broth and salt in Instant Pot®; slowly whisk in polenta until blended.

2. Secure lid and move pressure release valve to Sealing position. Press Manual; cook at high pressure 5 minutes.

3. When cooking is complete, use natural release for 5 minutes, then release remaining pressure.

4. Whisk in ½ cup cheese and butter until well blended. (Polenta may appear separated immediately after cooking but will come together when stirred.) Serve with additional cheese; garnish with sage.

MAKES 6 SERVINGS

TIP: Spread any leftover polenta in a baking dish and refrigerate until cold. Cut the cold polenta into sticks or slices, brush with olive oil and pan-fry or grill until lightly browned.

1 tablespoon vegetable oil

1½ pounds boneless skinless chicken breasts

2 medium onions, chopped

1 can (4 ounces) diced mild green chiles

1 tablespoon minced garlic

2 teaspoons ground cumin

1 teaspoon salt

1 teaspoon dried oregano

¼ teaspoon black pepper

¼ teaspoon ground red pepper

1½ cups chicken broth

2 cans (about 15 ounces each) Great Northern beans, rinsed and drained

¼ cup chopped fresh cilantro

1. Press Sauté; heat oil in Instant Pot®. Add chicken; cook about 6 minutes or until browned on both sides. Remove to plate. Add onion and chiles to pot; cook and stir 3 minutes. Add garlic, cumin, salt, oregano, black pepper and red pepper; cook and stir 1 minute. Stir in broth, scraping up browned bits from bottom of pot. Stir in beans. Return chicken to pot, pressing into liquid.

2. Secure lid and move pressure release valve to Sealing position. Press Manual; cook at high pressure 7 minutes.

3. When cooking is complete, press Cancel and use quick release. Remove chicken to clean plate; set aside until cool enough to handle.

4. Shred chicken into bite-size pieces; return to pot. Press Sauté; cook 2 to 3 minutes or until chili thickens slightly. Sprinkle with cilantro.

MAKES 6 SERVINGS

EASY HERBED RICE

1½ cups uncooked
    long grain rice

1½ cups water

2 tablespoons minced
    onion

2 tablespoons butter

1 clove garlic, minced

½ teaspoon salt

2 tablespoons minced
    fresh parsley

2 tablespoons minced
    fresh basil *or* 1 teaspoon
    dried basil*

2 tablespoons minced fresh
    oregano *or* 1 teaspoon
    dried oregano*

**If using dried herbs, add to
rice before cooking.*

1. Rinse rice well; drain in fine-mesh strainer. Combine rice, water, onion, butter, garlic and salt in Instant Pot®; mix well.

2. Secure lid and move pressure release valve to Sealing position. Press Manual; cook at high pressure 4 minutes.

3. When cooking is complete, use natural release for 10 minutes, then release remaining pressure.

4. Stir in parsley, basil and oregano. Fluff rice gently with fork before serving.

MAKES 4 TO 6 SERVINGS

TIP: To make this recipe with brown rice, cook at high pressure 22 minutes.

Sweet Potato and Black Bean Chili *(page 176)*

Colcannon *(page 181)*

Parmesan Potato Wedges *(page 157)*

VEGETABLES

Orange-Spiced Glazed Carrots *(page 152)*

French Onion Soup *(page 160)*

Shakshuka *(page 186)*

Easy Corn Chowder *(page 151)*

VEGETABLES

1 tablespoon olive oil

1 onion, chopped

1 clove garlic, minced

1 teaspoon salt

½ teaspoon ground turmeric

½ teaspoon ground cumin

¼ teaspoon paprika

¼ teaspoon ground red pepper

¼ teaspoon ground cinnamon

1 medium butternut squash, peeled and cut into 1-inch cubes

1 medium eggplant, cut into 1-inch cubes (about 4 cups)

1 can (about 15 ounces) chickpeas, rinsed and drained

1 can (about 14 ounces) vegetable broth

1 package (10 ounces) frozen cut okra

1 medium carrot, sliced

1 medium tomato, chopped

1 can (8 ounces) tomato sauce

⅓ cup raisins

2 cups sliced zucchini

Hot cooked couscous or rice

Chopped fresh parsley (optional)

1. Press Sauté; heat oil in Instant Pot®. Add onion; cook and stir 3 minutes or until softened. Add garlic, salt, turmeric, cumin, paprika, red pepper and cinnamon; cook and stir 30 seconds. Add butternut squash, eggplant, chickpeas, broth, okra, carrot, tomato, tomato sauce and raisins; mix well.

2. Secure lid and move pressure release valve to Sealing position. Press Manual; cook at high pressure 5 minutes.

3. When cooking is complete, press Cancel and use quick release.

4. Press Sauté; add zucchini to pot. Cook 3 minutes or until zucchini is tender, stirring occasionally. Serve over couscous; garnish with parsley.

MAKES 6 SERVINGS

COCONUT BUTTERNUT SQUASH

1 tablespoon butter

½ cup chopped onion

1 butternut squash (about 3 pounds), peeled and cut into 1-inch pieces

1 can (about 13 ounces) coconut milk*

1 to 2 tablespoons packed brown sugar, divided

1¼ teaspoons salt

½ teaspoon ground cinnamon

¼ teaspoon ground nutmeg

¼ teaspoon ground allspice

2 teaspoons grated fresh ginger

2 tablespoons lemon juice

Shake vigorously before opening to mix thoroughly.

1. Press Sauté; melt butter in Instant Pot®. Add onion; cook and stir 2 minutes. Add squash, coconut milk, 1 tablespoon brown sugar, salt, cinnamon, nutmeg and allspice; mix well.

2. Secure lid and move pressure release valve to Sealing position. Press Manual; cook at high pressure 6 minutes.

3. When cooking is complete, press Cancel and use quick release.

4. Stir ginger into squash mixture. Use immersion blender to blend squash until smooth. (Or process in food processor or blender.) Stir in lemon juice. Sprinkle individual servings with remaining 1 tablespoon brown sugar, if desired.

MAKES 4 TO 6 SERVINGS

SWEET AND SOUR RED CABBAGE

2 slices thick-cut bacon, chopped

1 cup chopped onion

1 head red cabbage (2 to 3 pounds), thinly sliced (about 8 cups)

1 pound unpeeled Granny Smith apples, cut into ½-inch pieces (about 2 medium)

½ cup honey

½ cup cider vinegar

¼ cup plus 3 tablespoons water, divided

1 teaspoon salt

1 teaspoon celery salt

¼ teaspoon black pepper

2 tablespoons all-purpose flour

1. Press Sauté; cook bacon in Instant Pot® until crisp. Remove to paper towel-lined plate.

2. Add onion to pot; cook and stir 3 minutes or until softened. Stir in cabbage, apples, honey, vinegar, ¼ cup water, salt, celery salt and pepper; mix well.

3. Secure lid and move pressure release valve to Sealing position. Press Manual; cook at high pressure 5 minutes.

4. When cooking is complete, use natural release for 10 minutes, then release remaining pressure.

5. Stir remaining 3 tablespoons water into flour in small bowl until smooth. Press Sauté; add flour mixture to pot. Cook and stir about 3 minutes or until sauce thickens. Sprinkle with bacon; serve warm.

MAKES 8 SERVINGS

QUICK VEGETABLE CURRY

2 teaspoons salt

2 teaspoons curry powder

1 teaspoon cumin seeds

1 teaspoon ground
    coriander

¼ teaspoon ground turmeric

¼ teaspoon ground
    red pepper

1 tablespoon vegetable oil

1 large onion, finely
    chopped

4 cloves garlic, minced

1 tablespoon grated
    fresh ginger

¼ cup tomato paste

1 cup water

1 head cauliflower
    (about 1 pound),
    broken into florets

2 baking potatoes,
    peeled and cut
    into ½-inch pieces

1 red bell pepper, cut
    into ½-inch pieces

2 carrots, cut into
    ¼-inch pieces

1 package (12 ounces)
    frozen peas, thawed

1. Combine salt, curry powder, cumin seeds, coriander, turmeric and ground red pepper in small bowl; mix well.

2. Press Sauté; heat oil in Instant Pot®. Add onion; cook and stir 3 minutes or until softened. Add garlic, ginger and spice mixture; cook and stir 1 minute. Add tomato paste; cook and stir 30 seconds. Stir in water, scraping up browned bits from bottom of pot. Add cauliflower, potatoes, bell pepper and carrots; stir to coat with sauce.

3. Secure lid and move pressure release valve to Sealing position. Press Manual; cook at high pressure 2 minutes.

4. When cooking is complete, press Cancel and use quick release.

5. Stir in peas; let stand 2 to 3 minutes or until heated through.

MAKES 6 TO 8 SERVINGS

EASY CORN CHOWDER

6 slices bacon, chopped

1 medium onion, diced

1 red bell pepper, diced

1 stalk celery, sliced

1 package (16 ounces) frozen corn, thawed

3 small potatoes, peeled and cut into ½-inch pieces (about 2 cups)

½ teaspoon ground coriander

3 cups chicken broth

½ teaspoon salt

½ teaspoon black pepper

¼ teaspoon ground red pepper

½ cup whipping cream

1. Press Sauté; cook bacon in Instant Pot® until crisp. Remove to paper towel-lined plate. Drain off all but 1 tablespoon drippings.

2. Add onion, bell pepper and celery to pot; cook and stir 3 minutes or until vegetables are softened. Add corn, potatoes and coriander; cook and stir 1 minute. Stir in broth, salt, black pepper and ground red pepper; mix well.

3. Secure lid and move pressure release valve to Sealing position. Press Manual; cook at high pressure 4 minutes.

4. When cooking is complete, use natural release for 10 minutes, then release remaining pressure.

5. Press Sauté; cook 2 to 3 minutes or until soup thickens, partially mashing potatoes. Stir in cream; cook until heated through. Top with bacon.

MAKES 4 SERVINGS

ORANGE-SPICED GLAZED CARROTS

1 package (32 ounces) baby carrots

½ cup orange juice

⅓ cup packed brown sugar

3 tablespoons butter, cut into small pieces

¾ teaspoon ground cinnamon

½ teaspoon salt

¼ teaspoon ground nutmeg

¼ cup water

2 tablespoons cornstarch

Grated orange peel (optional)

Chopped fresh parsley (optional)

1. Combine carrots, orange juice, brown sugar, butter, cinnamon, salt and nutmeg in Instant Pot®; mix well.

2. Secure lid and move pressure release valve to Sealing position. Press Manual; cook at high pressure 2 minutes.

3. When cooking is complete, press Cancel and use quick release.

4. Stir water into cornstarch in small bowl until smooth. Press Sauté; add cornstarch mixture to pot. Cook and stir 1 to 2 minutes or until sauce thickens. Garnish with orange peel and parsley.

MAKES 6 SERVINGS

CAULIFLOWER BISQUE

1 head cauliflower (about 1½ pounds), broken into florets

1 large baking potato (about 1 pound), peeled and cut into 1-inch pieces

2 cans (about 14 ounces each) vegetable or chicken broth

1 cup chopped onion

1 clove garlic, minced

1 teaspoon salt

½ teaspoon dried thyme

⅛ teaspoon ground red pepper (optional)

⅛ teaspoon black pepper

1 can (5 ounces) evaporated milk

2 tablespoons butter

1 cup (4 ounces) shredded Cheddar cheese

¼ cup finely chopped fresh parsley

¼ cup finely chopped green onions

1. Combine cauliflower, potato, broth, onion, garlic, salt, thyme, red pepper, if desired, and black pepper in Instant Pot®; mix well.

2. Secure lid and move pressure release valve to Sealing position. Press Manual; cook at high pressure 5 minutes.

3. When cooking is complete, use natural release for 10 minutes, then release remaining pressure.

4. Use immersion blender to blend soup in pot until smooth (or process soup in batches in food processor or blender). Stir in evaporated milk and butter until blended. Top with cheese, parsley and green onions.

MAKES 6 SERVINGS

CIDER VINAIGRETTE-GLAZED BEETS

6 medium red and/or
   golden beets
   (about 3 pounds)

1 cup water

2 tablespoons cider vinegar

1 tablespoon extra virgin
  olive oil

1 teaspoon Dijon mustard

½ teaspoon packed
  brown sugar

¾ teaspoon salt

¼ teaspoon black pepper

⅓ cup crumbled blue cheese
  (optional)

1. Cut tops off beets, leaving at least 1 inch of stems. Scrub beets under cold running water with soft vegetable brush, being careful not to break skins. Pour 1 cup water into Instant Pot®. Place rack in pot; place beets on rack (or use steamer basket to hold beets).

2. Secure lid and move pressure release valve to Sealing position. Press Manual; cook at high pressure 22 minutes.

3. When cooking is complete, use natural release for 10 minutes, then release remaining pressure. Check doneness by inserting paring knife into beets; knife should go in easily. If not, cook an additional 2 to 4 minutes.

4. Whisk vinegar, oil, mustard, brown sugar, salt and pepper in medium bowl until well blended.

5. When beets are cool enough to handle, peel off skins and trim root ends. Cut into wedges. Add warm beets to vinaigrette; toss gently to coat. Sprinkle with cheese, if desired. Serve warm or at room temperature.

MAKES 6 SERVINGS

TIP: The cooking time depends on the size of the beets, which can vary slightly. If beets are not tender enough, secure lid and cook under pressure 2 to 4 minutes longer.

MASHED ROOT VEGETABLES

1 pound baking potatoes, peeled and cut into 1-inch pieces

1 pound turnips, peeled and cut into 1-inch pieces

12 ounces sweet potatoes, peeled and cut into 1-inch pieces

8 ounces parsnips, peeled and cut into ½-inch pieces

¼ cup (½ stick) butter, cubed

⅓ cup water

2 teaspoons salt

¼ teaspoon black pepper

½ cup milk

1. Combine baking potatoes, turnips, sweet potatoes, parsnips, butter, water, salt and pepper in Instant Pot®; mix well.

2. Secure lid and move pressure release valve to Sealing position. Press Manual; cook at high pressure 10 minutes.

3. When cooking is complete, press Cancel and use quick release.

4. Mash vegetables with potato masher until almost smooth. Press Sauté; stir in milk until blended. Cook and stir about 3 minutes or until milk is absorbed and vegetables reach desired consistency.

MAKES 6 SERVINGS

SPICY ASIAN GREEN BEANS

1 cup water

1 pound fresh green beans, trimmed

2 tablespoons chopped green onions

2 tablespoons dry sherry or chicken broth

1½ tablespoons soy sauce

1 teaspoon chili sauce with garlic

1 teaspoon dark sesame oil

1 clove garlic, minced

1. Pour water into Instant Pot®. Place rack in pot; place beans on rack. (Arrange beans perpendicular to rack to prevent beans from falling through.)

2. Secure lid and move pressure release valve to Sealing position. Press Manual; cook at high pressure 2 minutes.

3. When cooking is complete, press Cancel and use quick release. Remove rack from pot; drain off and discard cooking liquid. Place beans in large bowl.

4. Press Sauté; add green onions, sherry, soy sauce, chili sauce, oil and garlic to pot. Cook and stir 1 to 2 minutes or until heated through.

5. Pour sauce over beans; toss to coat.

MAKES 4 SERVINGS

PARMESAN POTATO WEDGES

2 pounds red potatoes (about 6 medium), cut into ½-inch wedges

½ cup water

¼ cup finely chopped onion

2 tablespoons butter, cut into pieces

1¼ teaspoons salt

1 teaspoon dried oregano

¼ teaspoon black pepper

¼ cup grated Parmesan cheese

1. Combine potatoes, water, onion, butter, salt, oregano and pepper in Instant Pot®; mix well.

2. Secure lid and move pressure release valve to Sealing position. Press Manual; cook at high pressure 3 minutes.

3. When cooking is complete, press Cancel and use quick release.

4. Transfer potatoes to serving platter; sprinkle with cheese.

MAKES 4 TO 6 SERVINGS

VEGETABLE BEAN SOUP

1 cup dried Great Northern beans, soaked 8 hours or overnight

1 tablespoon olive oil

1 cup chopped onion

¾ cup chopped carrots

3 cloves garlic, minced

4 cups coarsely chopped green cabbage

4 cups coarsely chopped unpeeled red potatoes (about 4 medium)

1 teaspoon dried rosemary

4 cups vegetable broth

1 can (about 14 ounces) diced tomatoes

1½ teaspoons salt

½ teaspoon black pepper

Grated Parmesan cheese (optional)

1. Rinse and drain beans. Press Sauté; heat oil in Instant Pot®. Add onion and carrots; cook and stir 3 minutes or until vegetables are softened. Add garlic; cook and stir 30 seconds. Add cabbage, potatoes and rosemary; cook and stir 1 minute. Stir in beans, broth, tomatoes, salt and pepper; mix well.

2. Secure lid and move pressure release valve to Sealing position. Press Manual; cook at high pressure 7 minutes.

3. When cooking is complete, use natural release for 10 minutes, then release remaining pressure. Serve with cheese, if desired.

MAKES 6 TO 8 SERVINGS

LEMON PARMESAN CAULIFLOWER

1 cup water

3 tablespoons chopped fresh parsley

½ teaspoon grated lemon peel

1 large head cauliflower (2 to 3 pounds), trimmed

1 tablespoon butter

3 cloves garlic, minced

2 tablespoons lemon juice

½ teaspoon salt

¼ cup grated Parmesan cheese

1. Pour water into Instant Pot®; stir in parsley and lemon peel. Place rack in pot; place cauliflower on rack.

2. Secure lid and move pressure release valve to Sealing position. Press Manual; cook at high pressure 3 minutes.

3. When cooking is complete, press Cancel and use quick release. Remove rack from pot; place cauliflower in large bowl. Reserve ½ cup cooking liquid; discard remaining liquid.

4. Press Sauté; heat butter in pot. Add garlic; cook and stir 1 minute or until fragrant. Add lemon juice, salt and reserved ½ cup cooking liquid; cook and stir until heated through.

5. Spoon lemon sauce over cauliflower; sprinkle with cheese. Cut into wedges to serve.

MAKES 6 SERVINGS

FRENCH ONION SOUP

¼ cup (½ stick) butter

4 medium yellow onions (about 3 pounds), sliced

1 tablespoon sugar

¾ teaspoon salt

¼ teaspoon black pepper

¼ cup dry white wine or sherry

8 cups beef broth

8 to 16 slices French bread

1 cup (4 ounces) shredded Gruyère or Swiss cheese

1. Press Sauté; melt butter in Instant Pot®. Add onions; cook 15 minutes, stirring occasionally. Add sugar, salt and pepper; cook and stir 5 to 7 minutes or until onions are golden brown. Add wine; cook and stir 1 minute or until evaporated. Stir in broth; mix well.

2. Secure lid and move pressure release valve to Sealing position. Press Manual; cook at high pressure 5 minutes.

3. When cooking is complete, press Cancel and use quick release. Preheat broiler.

4. Ladle soup into individual ovenproof bowls; top with 1 or 2 slices bread and about 2 tablespoons cheese. Place bowls on large baking sheet. Broil 1 to 2 minutes or until bread is toasted and cheese is melted and browned.

MAKES 8 SERVINGS

FALL VEGETABLE MEDLEY

2 medium Yukon Gold potatoes, peeled and cut into ½-inch pieces

2 medium sweet potatoes, peeled and cut into ½-inch pieces

3 parsnips, peeled and cut into ½-inch pieces

1 bulb fennel, cut into ½-inch pieces

½ cup chopped fresh parsley

2 tablespoons butter, cut into small pieces

⅔ cup chicken or vegetable broth

2 teaspoons salt

½ teaspoon black pepper

1. Combine Yukon Gold potatoes, sweet potatoes, parsnips, fennel, parsley and butter in Instant Pot®.

2. Combine broth, salt and pepper in measuring cup or small bowl; mix well. Pour over vegetables; stir gently to coat.

3. Secure lid and move pressure release valve to Sealing position. Press Manual; cook at high pressure 4 minutes.

4. When cooking is complete, press Cancel and use quick release.

5. Gently stir vegetables. If some liquid remains in bottom of pot, press Sauté and cook 2 to 3 minutes or until liquid has evaporated.

MAKES 6 SERVINGS

POTATO AND LEEK SOUP

8 ounces bacon, chopped

1 leek, chopped

1 onion, chopped

2 carrots, diced

4 cups chicken broth

3 potatoes, peeled
   and diced

1½ cups chopped cabbage

1½ teaspoons salt

½ teaspoon caraway seeds

½ teaspoon black pepper

1 bay leaf

½ cup sour cream

Chopped fresh parsley
   (optional)

1. Press Sauté; cook bacon in Instant Pot® until crisp. Remove to paper towel-lined plate. Drain off all but 2 tablespoons drippings.

2. Add leek, onion and carrots to pot; cook and stir about 3 minutes or until vegetables are softened. Stir in broth, scraping up browned bits from bottom of pot. Stir in potatoes, cabbage, salt, caraway seeds, pepper and bay leaf; mix well.

3. Secure lid and move pressure release valve to Sealing position. Press Manual; cook at high pressure 4 minutes.

4. When cooking is complete, use natural release for 10 minutes, then release remaining pressure. Remove and discard bay leaf.

5. Whisk ½ cup hot soup into sour cream in small bowl until blended. Add sour cream mixture and bacon to soup; mix well. Garnish with parsley.

MAKES 6 SERVINGS

SUMMER SQUASH LASAGNA

2 tablespoons olive oil

1 onion, chopped

1 medium zucchini, cut crosswise into ¼-inch slices

1 medium yellow squash, cut crosswise into ¼-inch slices

2 cloves garlic, minced

1 teaspoon salt, divided

1 cup ricotta cheese

1½ cups (6 ounces) shredded mozzarella cheese, divided

½ cup grated Parmesan cheese, divided

¼ cup plus 2 tablespoons chopped fresh basil, divided

1 egg

¼ teaspoon black pepper

2¼ cups marinara sauce

8 oven-ready (no-boil) lasagna noodles

1 cup water

1. Spray 7-inch springform pan with nonstick cooking spray; set aside. Heat oil in large skillet over medium-high heat. Add onion, zucchini and yellow squash; cook and stir about 5 minutes or until vegetables are softened and lightly browned. Add garlic and ½ teaspoon salt; cook and stir 30 seconds.

2. Combine ricotta, ¼ cup mozzarella, ¼ cup Parmesan, ¼ cup basil, egg, remaining ½ teaspoon salt and pepper in medium bowl; mix well.

3. Spread ¼ cup marinara sauce in bottom of prepared springform pan. Layer with 2 noodles, breaking to fit. Spread one third of ricotta mixture over noodles. Top with one third of vegetables, ¼ cup mozzarella and ½ cup sauce. Repeat layers twice. For final layer, top with remaining 2 noodles, ½ cup sauce, ½ cup mozzarella and ¼ cup Parmesan. Cover pan tightly with foil.

4. Pour water into Instant Pot®. Place pan on rack; lower rack into pot. Secure lid and move pressure release valve to Sealing position. Press Manual; cook at high pressure 20 minutes.

5. When cooking is complete, use natural release. Carefully remove pan from pot. Remove foil.

6. If desired, preheat broiler; broil lasagna 1 minute or until cheese is browned. Cool in pan 10 minutes. Remove side of pan; sprinkle with remaining 2 tablespoons basil. Cut into squares or wedges.

MAKES 4 TO 6 SERVINGS

SPICED SWEET POTATOES

2½ pounds sweet potatoes, peeled and cut into ½-inch pieces

½ cup water

2 tablespoons dark brown sugar

1 teaspoon salt

1 teaspoon ground cinnamon

½ teaspoon ground nutmeg

2 tablespoons butter, cut into small pieces

½ teaspoon vanilla

1. Combine sweet potatoes, water, brown sugar, salt, cinnamon and nutmeg in Instant Pot®; mix well.

2. Secure lid and move pressure release valve to Sealing position. Press Manual; cook at high pressure 3 minutes.

3. When cooking is complete, press Cancel and use quick release.

4. Press Sauté; add butter and vanilla to pot. Cook 1 to 2 minutes or until butter is melted, stirring gently to blend.

MAKES 4 TO 6 SERVINGS

EGGPLANT ITALIANO

1 tablespoon olive oil

2 medium onions, thinly sliced

1¼ pounds eggplant, cut into 1-inch cubes

2 medium stalks celery, cut into 1-inch pieces

1 can (about 14 ounces) diced tomatoes

½ cup pitted black olives, sliced

3 tablespoons tomato sauce

2 tablespoons balsamic vinegar

1 tablespoon sugar

1 tablespoon capers, drained

1 teaspoon dried oregano or basil

¾ teaspoon salt

¼ teaspoon black pepper

1. Press Sauté; heat oil in Instant Pot®. Add onions; cook and stir 3 minutes or until softened. Add eggplant, celery, tomatoes, olives, tomato sauce, vinegar, sugar, capers, oregano, salt and pepper; mix well.

2. Secure lid and move pressure release valve to Sealing position. Press Manual; cook at high pressure 2 minutes.

3. When cooking is complete, press Cancel and use quick release.

MAKES 6 SERVINGS

SOUTHWESTERN CORN AND BEANS

2 cups dried kidney beans, soaked 8 hours or overnight

1 tablespoon olive oil

1 large onion, chopped

1 jalapeño pepper, minced

1 clove garlic, minced

2 teaspoons chili powder

½ teaspoon ground cumin

1 can (about 14 ounces) diced tomatoes

1 green bell pepper, cut into 1-inch pieces

½ cup water

1½ teaspoons salt

½ teaspoon black pepper

1 package (16 ounces) frozen corn, thawed

1. Drain and rinse beans. Press Sauté; heat oil in Instant Pot®. Add onion; cook and stir 3 minutes or until softened. Add jalapeño, garlic, chili powder and cumin; cook and stir 1 minute. Add tomatoes, bell pepper, water, salt and black pepper; mix well. Stir in beans.

2. Secure lid and move pressure release valve to Sealing position. Press Manual; cook at high pressure 25 minutes.

3. When cooking is complete, use natural release for 10 minutes, then release remaining pressure.

4. Press Sauté; stir in corn. Cook about 5 minutes or until mixture thickens and corn is heated through, stirring occasionally.

MAKES 6 SERVINGS

SPICY SQUASH AND CHICKEN SOUP

1 tablespoon
vegetable oil

1 small onion,
finely chopped

1 stalk celery,
finely chopped

2 cups chicken broth

2 cups cubed
butternut squash
(1-inch pieces)

1 can (about
14 ounces) diced
tomatoes with
chiles

8 ounces boneless
skinless chicken
thighs, cut into
½-inch pieces

½ teaspoon salt

½ teaspoon
ground ginger

⅛ teaspoon
ground cumin

⅛ teaspoon
black pepper

2 teaspoons
lime juice

½ to 1 teaspoon hot
pepper sauce

Fresh cilantro or
parsley sprigs
(optional)

1. Press Sauté; heat oil in Instant Pot®. Add onion and celery; cook and stir 4 minutes or until vegetables are softened. Add broth, squash, tomatoes, chicken, salt, ginger, cumin and black pepper; mix well.

2. Secure lid and move pressure release valve to Sealing position. Press Manual; cook at high pressure 5 minutes.

3. When cooking is complete, use natural release for 10 minutes, then release remaining pressure.

4. Stir in lime juice and hot pepper sauce; garnish with cilantro.

MAKES 4 SERVINGS

FENNEL BRAISED WITH TOMATO

2 bulbs fennel

1 tablespoon olive oil

1 small onion, sliced

1 clove garlic, minced

3 tablespoons dry white wine

4 medium tomatoes, chopped

⅓ cup vegetable broth or water

1 tablespoon chopped fresh marjoram *or* 1 teaspoon dried marjoram

½ teaspoon salt

¼ teaspoon black pepper

1. Trim stems and bottoms from fennel bulbs, reserving fronds for garnish. Cut each bulb lengthwise into 4 wedges.

2. Press Sauté; heat oil in Instant Pot®. Add fennel, onion and garlic; cook and stir 5 minutes or until onion is translucent. Add wine; cook and stir until almost evaporated. Stir in tomatoes, broth, marjoram, salt and pepper; mix well.

3. Secure lid and move pressure release valve to Sealing position. Press Manual; cook at high pressure 4 minutes.

4. When cooking is complete, use natural release for 10 minutes, then release remaining pressure. Transfer vegetables to medium bowl with slotted spoon.

5. Press Sauté; cook liquid remaining in pot about 5 minutes or until reduced by one third. Add to vegetables; mix well. Garnish with reserved fennel fronds.

MAKES 6 SERVINGS

BALSAMIC GREEN BEANS WITH ALMONDS

1 cup water

1 pound fresh green beans, trimmed

1 tablespoon extra virgin olive oil

2 teaspoons balsamic vinegar

½ teaspoon salt

¼ teaspoon black pepper

2 tablespoons sliced almonds, toasted*

*To toast almonds, cook in small skillet over medium heat 1 to 2 minutes or until lightly browned, stirring frequently.

1. Pour water into Instant Pot®. Place rack in pot; place beans on rack. (Arrange beans perpendicular to rack to prevent beans from falling through.)

2. Secure lid and move pressure release valve to Sealing position. Press Manual; cook at high pressure 2 minutes.

3. When cooking is complete, press Cancel and use quick release. Remove rack from pot; place beans in large bowl.

4. Add oil, vinegar, salt and pepper; toss to coat. Sprinkle with almonds just before serving.

MAKES 4 SERVINGS

CARIBBEAN SWEET POTATOES

2½ pounds sweet potatoes, peeled and cut into 1-inch pieces

8 ounces shredded peeled carrots

¾ cup flaked coconut, divided

½ cup water

¼ cup (½ stick) butter, cut into small pieces

3 tablespoons sugar

1 teaspoon salt

½ cup chopped walnuts, toasted*

2 tablespoons lime juice

1 teaspoon grated lime peel

To toast walnuts, cook in small skillet over medium heat 6 to 8 minutes or until fragrant, stirring frequently.

1. Combine sweet potatoes, carrots, ½ cup coconut, water, butter and salt in Instant Pot®; mix well.

2. Secure lid and move pressure release valve to Sealing position. Press Manual; cook at high pressure 5 minutes. Meanwhile, place remaining ¼ cup coconut in small skillet; cook 4 minutes or until lightly browned, stirring frequently.

3. When cooking is complete, press Cancel and use quick release.

4. Mash sweet potatoes in pot until desired consistency. Stir in walnuts, lime juice and lime peel until blended. Sprinkle with toasted coconut.

MAKES 6 TO 8 SERVINGS

POTATO SOUP WITH GREEN CHILES AND CHEESE

1 tablespoon
  vegetable oil

1 medium onion,
  chopped

1 clove garlic, minced

1 tablespoon
  all-purpose flour

2 cups chopped
  unpeeled potatoes

2 cups chicken broth

½ teaspoon salt

½ teaspoon celery
  salt, divided

2 cups milk

1 can (4 ounces)
  diced green chiles,
  drained

¾ cup (3 ounces)
  shredded
  Monterey Jack
  cheese

¾ cup (3 ounces)
  shredded Colby or
  Cheddar cheese

1. Press Sauté; heat oil in Instant Pot®. Add onion and garlic; cook and stir 3 minutes or until softened. Stir in flour until blended. Add potatoes, broth, salt and ¼ teaspoon celery salt; mix well.

2. Secure lid and move pressure release valve to Sealing position. Press Manual; cook at high pressure 4 minutes.

3. When cooking is complete, press Cancel and use quick release.

4. Press Sauté; adjust heat to low ("less"). Add milk, chiles and remaining ¼ teaspoon celery salt; cook 5 minutes, stirring occasionally. Add Monterey Jack and Colby cheeses; cook and stir just until cheeses are melted. (Do not boil.)

MAKES 4 TO 6 SERVINGS

BEEF AND BEET BORSCHT

6 slices bacon, chopped

1½ pounds boneless beef chuck roast, trimmed and cut into ½-inch pieces

1 medium onion, chopped

4 cloves garlic, minced

4 medium beets, peeled and cut into ½-inch pieces

2 large carrots, sliced

2 cups beef broth

3 tablespoons honey

3 tablespoons red wine vinegar

6 sprigs fresh dill

2 bay leaves

3 cups shredded green cabbage

1. Press Sauté; cook bacon in Instant Pot® until crisp. Remove to paper towel-lined plate.

2. Add beef to pot; cook about 5 minutes or until browned. Remove to plate. Drain off all but 1 tablespoon fat. Add onion to pot; cook and stir 3 minutes or until softened. Add garlic; cook and stir 30 seconds. Add beets, carrots, broth, honey, vinegar, dill and bay leaves; mix well.

3. Secure lid and move pressure release valve to Sealing position. Press Manual; cook at high pressure 25 minutes.

4. When cooking is complete, use natural release for 15 minutes, then release remaining pressure. Add cabbage to pot. Secure lid and move pressure release valve to Sealing position. Press Manual; cook at high pressure 1 minute.

5. When cooking is complete, press Cancel and use quick release. Remove and discard dill stems and bay leaves.

MAKES 6 TO 8 SERVINGS

CURRIED CAULIFLOWER AND POTATOES

3 tablespoons vegetable oil

1 medium onion, chopped

1 tablespoon minced garlic

1 tablespoon curry powder

1½ teaspoons salt

1½ teaspoons grated fresh ginger

1 teaspoon ground turmeric

1 teaspoon yellow or brown mustard seeds

¼ teaspoon red pepper flakes

½ cup water

1 medium head cauliflower, cut into 1-inch pieces

1½ pounds fingerling potatoes, cut into halves

1. Press Sauté; heat oil in Instant Pot®. Add onion; cook and stir about 6 minutes or until beginning to brown. Add garlic, curry powder, salt, ginger, turmeric, mustard seeds and red pepper flakes; cook and stir 1 minute. Stir in water, scraping up browned bits from bottom of pot. Stir in cauliflower and potatoes; mix well.

2. Secure lid and move pressure release valve to Sealing position. Press Manual; cook at high pressure 4 minutes.

3. When cooking is complete, press Cancel and use quick release.

MAKES 6 SERVINGS

BRUSSELS SPROUTS IN ORANGE SAUCE

½ cup plus 2 tablespoons orange juice, divided

½ teaspoon salt

¼ teaspoon red pepper flakes

¼ teaspoon ground cinnamon

¼ teaspoon black pepper

8 ounces fresh brussels sprouts (about 3 cups)

2 teaspoons cornstarch

1 teaspoon honey

1 teaspoon shredded or grated orange peel

1. Combine ½ cup orange juice, salt, red pepper flakes, cinnamon and black pepper in Instant Pot®; mix well. Stir in brussels sprouts.

2. Secure lid and move pressure release valve to Sealing position. Press Manual; cook at high pressure 2 minutes.

3. When cooking is complete, press Cancel and use quick release. Remove brussels sprouts to medium bowl with slotted spoon.

4. Stir remaining 2 tablespoons orange juice into cornstarch in small bowl until smooth. Press Sauté; add honey, orange peel and cornstarch mixture to pot. Cook 1 to 2 minutes or until sauce thickens, stirring constantly.

5. Pour sauce over brussels sprouts; stir gently to coat.

MAKES 4 SERVINGS

SPEEDY MINESTRONE

1 tablespoon olive oil

1 medium onion, chopped

3 medium carrots, chopped

3 stalks celery, chopped

2 cloves garlic, minced

1½ teaspoons salt

1 teaspoon Italian seasoning

¼ teaspoon black pepper

⅛ teaspoon red pepper flakes

2 russet potatoes (about 6 ounces each), peeled and cut into ½-inch pieces

2 cans (about 15 ounces each) cannellini beans, rinsed and drained

4 cups vegetable broth

1 can (about 14 ounces) diced tomatoes

1 bunch kale, stemmed and chopped (about 6 cups)

Shredded Parmesan cheese (optional)

1. Press Sauté; heat oil in Instant Pot®. Add onion, carrots, celery and garlic; cook and stir 5 minutes or until vegetables are softened. Add salt, Italian seasoning, black pepper and red pepper flakes; cook and stir 1 minute. Stir in potatoes, beans, broth and tomatoes; mix well.

2. Secure lid and move pressure release valve to Sealing position. Press Manual; cook at high pressure 3 minutes.

3. When cooking is complete, press Cancel and use quick release. Stir in kale. Secure lid and move pressure release valve to Sealing position. Press Manual; cook at high pressure 2 minutes.

4. When cooking is complete, use natural release for 5 minutes, then release remaining pressure. Serve with cheese, if desired.

MAKES 6 TO 8 SERVINGS

SWEET POTATO AND BLACK BEAN CHILI

1 tablespoon olive oil

1 large onion, chopped

4 teaspoons chili powder

2 cloves garlic, minced

1 teaspoon salt

1 teaspoon chipotle chili powder

½ teaspoon ground cumin

1½ cups vegetable broth or water

2 cans (about 15 ounces each) black beans, rinsed and drained

1 large sweet potato, peeled and cut into ½-inch pieces

1 can (about 14 ounces) diced tomatoes

1 can (about 14 ounces) crushed tomatoes

Optional toppings: sour cream, sliced green onions, shredded cheddar cheese and/or tortilla chips

1. Press Sauté; heat oil in Instant Pot®. Add onion; cook 3 minutes or until softened. Add chili powder, garlic, salt, chipotle chili powder and cumin; cook and stir 1 minute. Stir in broth, scraping up browned bits from bottom of pot. Add black beans, sweet potato, diced tomatoes and crushed tomatoes; mix well.

2. Secure lid and move pressure release valve to Sealing position. Press Manual; cook at high pressure 4 minutes.

3. When cooking is complete, press Cancel and use quick release.

4. Press Sauté; cook and stir 3 to 5 minutes or until thickened to desired consistency. Serve with desired toppings.

MAKES 6 SERVINGS

CURRIED PARSNIP SOUP

2 tablespoons butter or olive oil

1 medium yellow onion, chopped

2 stalks celery, diced

3 cloves garlic, minced

1 tablespoon salt

2 teaspoons curry powder

½ teaspoon grated fresh ginger

½ teaspoon black pepper

3 pounds parsnips, peeled and cut into 2-inch pieces

6 cups vegetable or chicken broth

Chopped fresh chives (optional)

1. Press Sauté; melt butter in Instant Pot®. Add onion and celery; cook and stir 5 minutes or until onion is translucent. Add garlic, salt, curry powder, ginger and pepper; cook and stir 1 minute. Stir in parsnips and broth; mix well.

2. Secure lid and move pressure release valve to Sealing position. Press Manual; cook at high pressure 10 minutes.

3. When cooking is complete, use natural release for 10 minutes, then release remaining pressure.

4. Use immersion blender to blend soup until smooth. (Or purée soup in batches in food processor or blender.) Garnish with chives.

MAKES 6 TO 8 SERVINGS

MEXICAN CORN BREAD PUDDING

1 can (14¾ ounces) cream-style corn

¾ cup yellow cornmeal

2 eggs

1 can (4 ounces) diced mild green chiles

2 tablespoons vegetable oil

2 tablespoons sugar

2 teaspoons baking powder

¾ teaspoon salt

1¼ cups water

½ cup (2 ounces) shredded Cheddar cheese

1. Spray 6- to 7-inch (1½-quart) soufflé dish or round baking dish that fits inside Instant Pot® with nonstick cooking spray.

2. Combine corn, cornmeal, eggs, chiles, oil, sugar, baking powder and salt in medium bowl; mix well. Pour into prepared dish. Cover dish tightly with foil.

3. Pour water into pot. Place soufflé dish on rack; lower rack into pot.

4. Secure lid and move pressure release valve to Sealing position. Press Manual; cook at high pressure 25 minutes.

5. When cooking is complete, use natural release for 10 minutes, then release remaining pressure. Uncover; sprinkle with cheese. Tent with foil; let stand 5 minutes or until cheese is melted.

MAKES 8 SERVINGS

ROASTED TOMATO-BASIL SOUP

1 tablespoon olive oil

1 medium onion, finely chopped

3 tablespoons tomato paste

1 tablespoon packed dark brown sugar

1 teaspoon salt

¼ teaspoon black pepper

¼ teaspoon ground allspice

1 can (28 ounces) whole tomatoes, chopped, juice reserved

2 cans (about 14 ounces each) fire-roasted diced tomatoes

2 cups vegetable broth

1 can (5 ounces) evaporated milk

¼ cup shredded fresh basil leaves

1. Press Sauté; heat oil in Instant Pot®. Add onion; cook and stir 10 minutes or until dark brown. Add tomato paste, brown sugar, salt, pepper and allspice; cook and stir 1 minute. Stir in whole tomatoes with juice, diced tomatoes and broth; mix well.

2. Secure lid and move pressure release valve to Sealing position. Press Manual; cook at high pressure 5 minutes.

3. When cooking is complete, use natural release for 20 minutes, then release remaining pressure.

4. Press Sauté; add evaporated milk and shredded basil to pot. Cook and stir 1 minute or until heated through.

MAKES 6 SERVINGS

THAI RED CURRY WITH TOFU

2 tablespoons vegetable oil

5 medium shallots, thinly sliced (about 1½ cups)

3 tablespoons Thai red curry paste

1 teaspoon minced garlic

1 teaspoon grated fresh ginger

1 can (about 13 ounces) unsweetened coconut milk

1 medium sweet potato, peeled and cut into 1-inch pieces

1 small eggplant or large zucchini, halved lengthwise and cut crosswise into ½-inch-wide slices

1½ tablespoons soy sauce

1 tablespoon packed brown sugar

1 package (14 to 16 ounces) extra firm tofu, cut into 1-inch pieces

1 red bell pepper, cut into ¼-inch strips

½ cup green beans (1-inch pieces)

¼ cup chopped fresh basil

2 tablespoons lime juice

Hot cooked rice (optional)

1. Press Sauté; heat oil in Instant Pot®. Add shallots; cook and stir 2 minutes or until softened. Add curry paste, garlic and ginger; cook and stir 1 minute. Stir in coconut milk, sweet potato, eggplant, soy sauce and brown sugar; mix well.

2. Secure lid and move pressure release valve to Sealing position. Press Manual; cook at high pressure 4 minutes.

3. When cooking is complete, press Cancel and use quick release.

4. Add tofu, bell pepper and green beans to pot. Secure lid and move pressure release valve to Sealing position. Press Manual; cook at low pressure 1 minute.

5. When cooking is complete, press Cancel and use quick release. Stir in basil and lime juice. Serve over rice, if desired.

MAKES 4 SERVINGS

4 slices bacon

3 pounds russet potatoes, peeled and cut into 1-inch pieces

2 medium leeks, halved lengthwise and thinly sliced

½ cup water

1¼ teaspoons salt

¼ teaspoon black pepper

1 cup milk, divided

2 tablespoons butter, cut into pieces

½ small head savoy cabbage (about 1 pound), cored and thinly sliced (about 4 cups)

1. Press Sauté; cook bacon in Instant Pot® until crisp. Remove to paper towel-lined plate. Add potatoes, leeks, water, salt and pepper to pot; mix well.

2. Secure lid and move pressure release valve to Sealing position. Press Manual; cook at high pressure 5 minutes.

3. When cooking is complete, press Cancel and use quick release.

4. Press Sauté; add ½ cup milk and butter to pot. Cook and stir 1 minute, mashing potatoes until still slightly chunky. Add remaining ½ cup milk and cabbage; cook and stir 2 to 3 minutes or until cabbage is wilted. Stir in bacon.

MAKES 6 TO 8 SERVINGS

CREAMY CARROT SOUP

1 tablespoon butter

½ cup chopped onion

1 tablespoon chopped fresh ginger

1 pound baby carrots or regular carrots, cut into 2-inch pieces

½ teaspoon salt

¼ teaspoon black pepper

3 cups vegetable broth

¼ cup whipping cream

2 tablespoons orange juice

Pinch ground nutmeg

4 tablespoons sour cream (optional)

Fresh parsley sprigs (optional)

1. Press Sauté; melt butter in Instant Pot®. Add onion and ginger; cook and stir 1 minute or until ginger is fragrant. Add carrots, salt and pepper; cook and stir 2 minutes. Stir in broth; mix well.

2. Secure lid and move pressure release valve to Sealing position. Press Manual; cook at high pressure 6 minutes.

3. When cooking is complete, use natural release for 10 minutes, then release remaining pressure.

4. Use immersion blender to blend soup until smooth. (Or purée soup in batches in food processor or blender.)

5. Press Sauté; adjust heat to low ("less"). Add cream, orange juice and nutmeg; cook until heated through, stirring frequently. (Do not boil.) Top with sour cream and parsley, if desired.

MAKES 4 SERVINGS

LEMON-MINT RED POTATOES

2 pounds new
  red potatoes
  (1½ to 2 inches)

⅓ cup water

4 tablespoons
  chopped fresh
  mint, divided

1 tablespoon olive oil

1 teaspoon salt

1 teaspoon grated
  lemon peel

¾ teaspoon Greek
  seasoning or
  dried oregano

¼ teaspoon black
  pepper

1 tablespoon
  lemon juice

1 tablespoon butter

1. Combine potatoes, water, 2 tablespoons mint, oil, salt, lemon peel, Greek seasoning and pepper in Instant Pot®; mix well.

2. Secure lid and move pressure release valve to Sealing position. Press Manual; cook at high pressure 6 minutes.

3. When cooking is complete, press Cancel and use quick release.

4. Press Sauté; add remaining 2 tablespoons mint, lemon juice and butter to pot. Cook and stir 2 minutes or until butter is melted and potatoes are completely coated.

MAKES 4 SERVINGS

CORN AND SWEET POTATO CURRY

1 tablespoon vegetable oil

1 large onion, chopped

2 tablespoons minced fresh ginger

½ jalapeño pepper, seeded and minced

2 cloves garlic, minced

1 cup frozen corn

2 teaspoons curry powder

½ teaspoon salt

1 can (about 13 ounces) coconut milk, well shaken

1 tablespoon soy sauce

4 sweet potatoes, peeled and cut into ¾-inch cubes

Hot cooked jasmine or long grain rice

Chopped fresh cilantro and/or green onions (optional)

Chopped dry-roasted peanuts (optional)

1. Press Sauté; heat oil in Instant Pot®. Add onion, ginger, jalapeño and garlic; cook and stir 3 minutes or until softened. Add corn, curry powder and salt; cook and stir 1 minute. Add coconut milk and soy sauce; stir until well blended. Stir in sweet potatoes; mix well.

2. Secure lid and move pressure release valve to Sealing position. Press Manual; cook at high pressure 3 minutes.

3. When cooking is complete, press Cancel and use quick release.

4. Press Sauté; cook about 2 minutes or until sauce thickens slightly. Serve over rice; garnish with cilantro, green onions and peanuts.

MAKES 6 SERVINGS

RIBOLLITA (TUSCAN BREAD SOUP)

2 tablespoons olive oil

1 onion, halved and thinly sliced

2 stalks celery, diced

1 large carrot, julienned

3 cloves garlic, minced

1½ teaspoons salt

1 teaspoon Italian seasoning

1 bay leaf

¼ teaspoon black pepper

¼ teaspoon red pepper flakes (optional)

4 cups vegetable broth

1 can (28 ounces) whole tomatoes, coarsely chopped, juice reserved

1 can (about 15 ounces) cannellini beans, rinsed and drained

1 bunch kale, stemmed and coarsely chopped *or* 3 cups thinly sliced cabbage

8 ounces rustic Italian bread, cubed (½-inch pieces)

2 medium zucchini, thinly sliced

1 medium yellow squash, thinly sliced (⅛-inch slices)

Shredded Parmesan cheese (optional)

1. Press Sauté; heat oil in Instant Pot®. Add onion, celery and carrot; cook and stir 5 minutes. Add garlic, salt, Italian seasoning, bay leaf, black pepper and red pepper flakes, if desired; cook and stir 1 minute. Stir in broth, tomatoes with juice and beans; mix well.

2. Secure lid and move pressure release valve to Sealing position. Press Manual; cook at high pressure 8 minutes. When cooking is complete, press Cancel and use quick release.

3. Add kale, bread, zucchini and yellow squash to pot. Secure lid and move pressure release valve to Sealing position. Press Manual; cook at high pressure 1 minute.

4. When cooking is complete, press Cancel and use quick release. Serve with cheese, if desired.

MAKES 6 TO 8 SERVINGS

SHAKSHUKA

- 2 tablespoons extra virgin olive oil
- 1 large red bell pepper, chopped
- 1 medium onion, chopped
- 3 cloves garlic, minced
- 2 teaspoons sugar
- 2 teaspoons ground cumin
- 1 teaspoon paprika
- 1 teaspoon chili powder
- ½ teaspoon salt
- ¼ teaspoon red pepper flakes
- 1 can (28 ounces) crushed tomatoes
- ¾ cup crumbled feta cheese
- 4 eggs

1. Press Sauté; heat oil in Instant Pot®. Add bell pepper and onion; cook and stir 3 minutes or until softened. Add garlic, sugar, cumin, paprika, chili powder, salt and red pepper flakes; cook and stir 1 minute. Stir in tomatoes; mix well.

2. Secure lid and move pressure release valve to Sealing position. Press Manual; cook at high pressure 10 minutes.

3. When cooking is complete, press Cancel and use quick release.

4. Stir in cheese. Make four wells in sauce for eggs, leaving space between each. Slide eggs, one at a time, into wells in sauce. (For best results, crack each egg into small bowl before sliding into sauce.)

5. Secure lid and move pressure release valve to Sealing position. Press Manual; cook at low pressure 1 minute. When cooking is complete, press Cancel and use quick release. To cook eggs longer, press Sauté; cook until desired doneness.

MAKES 4 SERVINGS

CHUNKY RANCH POTATOES

3 pounds unpeeled red potatoes, quartered

½ cup water

1 teaspoon salt

½ cup ranch dressing

½ cup grated Parmesan cheese

¼ cup minced fresh chives

1. Combine potatoes, water and salt in Instant Pot®; mix well.

2. Secure lid and move pressure release valve to Sealing position. Press Manual; cook at high pressure 5 minutes.

3. When cooking is complete, press Cancel and use quick release.

4. Add ranch dressing, cheese and chives to pot; stir gently to coat, breaking potatoes into chunks.

MAKES 8 SERVINGS

VEGETABLE STOCK

8 cups water

2 large onions, tops and roots removed, brown outer skin intact, cut into wedges

6 medium carrots, cut into 2-inch pieces

3 stalks celery, cut into 2-inch pieces

6 sprigs fresh parsley

2 cloves garlic, crushed

2 bay leaves

1 teaspoon salt

4 whole black peppercorns

1. Combine water, onions, carrots, celery, parsley, garlic, bay leaves, salt and peppercorns in Instant Pot®; mix well.

2. Secure lid and move pressure release valve to Sealing position. Press Manual; cook at high pressure 30 minutes.

3. When cooking is complete, use natural release.

4. Strain stock into large bowl through fine-mesh strainer or colander lined with several layers of damp cheesecloth; discard solids. Stock can be refrigerated up to 3 days or frozen up to 3 months.

MAKES ABOUT 8 CUPS

Chocolate Orange Bread Pudding
(page 209)

Superfast Applesauce
(page 208)

Apple Spice Bread Pudding
(page 189)

DESSERTS

Warm Chocolate Cakes
(page 207)

Southern Sweet Potato Custard
(page 198)

Rich Chocolate Pudding
(page 194)

Brioche Rum Custard
(page 200)

DESSERTS

APPLE SPICE BREAD PUDDING

4 eggs

1 can (5 ounces) evaporated milk

½ cup packed brown sugar

¼ cup apple cider or apple juice

1 teaspoon ground cinnamon

½ teaspoon vanilla

¼ teaspoon salt

¼ teaspoon ground nutmeg

¼ teaspoon ground allspice

4 cups bread cubes

1½ cups cubed peeled Granny Smith apples (about 2 small)

½ cup chopped pecans

1¼ cups water

Ice cream (optional)

Caramel ice cream topping (optional)

1. Spray 6- to 7-inch (1½-quart) soufflé dish or round baking dish that fits inside Instant Pot® with nonstick cooking spray.

2. Whisk eggs, evaporated milk, brown sugar, apple cider, cinnamon, vanilla, salt, nutmeg and allspice in large bowl until well blended. Add bread cubes, apples and pecans; toss to coat. Pour into prepared dish; cover dish tightly with foil.

3. Pour water into pot. Place soufflé dish on rack; lower rack into pot.

4. Secure lid and move pressure release valve to Sealing position. Press Manual; cook at high pressure 40 minutes.

5. When cooking is complete, use natural release for 10 minutes, then release remaining pressure. Remove soufflé dish from pot. Remove foil; serve warm with ice cream and caramel topping, if desired.

MAKES 4 SERVINGS

VERY BERRY CHEESECAKE

CRUST

¾ cup honey graham cracker crumbs (about 5 whole crackers)

3 tablespoons butter, melted

CHEESECAKE

2 packages (8 ounces each) cream cheese, at room temperature

½ cup sugar

2 eggs, at room temperature

1 teaspoon vanilla

1 cup fresh blueberries*

1¼ cups water

TOPPING

½ cup seedless raspberry jam

1 cup fresh raspberries*

If blueberries or raspberries are unavailable, substitute seasonal berries or a mix of berries.

1. Cut parchment paper to fit bottom of 7-inch springform pan. Lightly spray bottom and side of pan with nonstick cooking spray. Wrap outside of pan with heavy-duty foil.

2. Combine graham cracker crumbs and melted butter in small bowl; mix well. Pat mixture onto bottom and about ½ inch up side of prepared pan. Freeze 10 minutes.

3. Beat cream cheese and sugar in large bowl with electric mixer at medium-high speed until light and fluffy. Add eggs, one at a time, beating well after each addition. Stir in vanilla. Sprinkle blueberries over crust; pour batter over blueberries. Cover pan tightly with foil.

4. Pour water into Instant Pot®. Place pan on rack; lower rack into pot. Secure lid and move pressure release valve to Sealing position. Press Manual; cook at high pressure 33 minutes.

5. When cooking is complete, press Cancel and use quick release. Use handles on rack to lift pan from pot. Remove foil; cool 1 hour. Run thin knife around edge of cheesecake to loosen (do not remove side of pan). Refrigerate 2 to 3 hours or overnight.

6. Remove side and bottom of pan; transfer cheesecake to serving plate, if desired. Heat jam in small saucepan over low heat or in glass measuring cup in microwave, stirring until smooth. Spoon melted jam over cheesecake; top with raspberries.

MAKES 6 TO 8 SERVINGS

CHOCOLATE RICE PUDDING

1 cup water

1 cup uncooked long grain rice

½ teaspoon salt, divided

1½ cups milk

½ cup sugar

2 tablespoons cornstarch

½ teaspoon vanilla

½ cup semisweet chocolate chips

Whipped cream (optional)

Chocolate curls (optional)

1. Combine water, rice and ¼ teaspoon salt in Instant Pot®; mix well.

2. Secure lid and move pressure release valve to Sealing position. Press Manual; cook at high pressure 4 minutes.

3. When cooking is complete, use natural release for 10 minutes, then release remaining pressure.

4. Whisk milk, sugar, cornstarch, vanilla and remaining ¼ teaspoon salt in medium bowl until well blended. Stir into cooked rice.

5. Press Sauté; cook and stir 5 minutes. Add chocolate chips; stir until melted and smooth. Garnish with whipped cream and chocolate curls.

MAKES 6 SERVINGS

APPLESAUCE CUSTARD

1½ cups unsweetened applesauce

½ teaspoon ground cinnamon

¼ teaspoon salt

4 eggs, at room temperature

½ cup half-and-half

¼ cup unsweetened apple juice concentrate

⅛ teaspoon ground nutmeg

1¼ cups water

1. Combine applesauce, cinnamon and salt in medium bowl; mix well. Whisk in eggs, half-and-half and apple juice concentrate until well blended. Pour into 1½-quart soufflé dish or round baking dish that fits inside Instant Pot®. Sprinkle with nutmeg. Cover dish tightly with foil.

2. Pour water into pot. Place soufflé dish on rack; lower rack into pot.

3. Secure lid and move pressure release valve to Sealing position. Press Manual; cook at high pressure 30 minutes.

4. When cooking is complete, use natural release for 10 minutes, then release remaining pressure.

5. Remove soufflé dish from pot. Remove foil; cool to room temperature. Serve custard at room temperature or chilled.

MAKES 6 SERVINGS

CHOCOLATE SURPRISE CRÈME BRÛLÉE

3 ounces bittersweet chocolate, finely chopped

5 egg yolks

1¾ cups whipping cream

½ cup granulated sugar

¼ teaspoon salt

1 teaspoon vanilla

1 cup water

¼ cup demerara or raw sugar

1. Spray bottoms of five 6-ounce ramekins or custard cups with nonstick cooking spray. Divide chocolate evenly among ramekins.

2. Whisk egg yolks in medium bowl. Combine cream, granulated sugar and salt in medium saucepan; bring to a simmer over medium heat. Slowly pour ¼ cup hot cream mixture into egg yolks, whisking until blended. Add remaining cream mixture in thin, steady stream, whisking constantly. Pour through fine-mesh strainer into clean bowl. Stir in vanilla. Ladle custard mixture into prepared ramekins over chocolate. Cover each ramekin tightly with foil.

3. Pour water into Instant Pot®; place rack in pot. Arrange ramekins on rack, stacking as necessary.

4. Secure lid and move pressure release valve to Sealing position. Press Manual; cook at high pressure 6 minutes.

5. When cooking is complete, use natural release for 10 minutes, then release remaining pressure. Remove ramekins from pot; cool to room temperature. Refrigerate until ready to serve.

6. Just before serving, preheat broiler. Place ramekins on baking sheet; sprinkle tops of custards with demerara sugar. Broil 4 inches from heat 1 to 2 minutes or until sugar bubbles and browns.

MAKES 5 SERVINGS

ESPRESSO CRÈME BRÛLÉE: Reduce cream to 1½ cups and add ¼ cup espresso. Heat mixture in saucepan with sugar and salt as directed in step 2.

RICH CHOCOLATE PUDDING

1½ cups whipping cream

4 ounces bittersweet chocolate, chopped

4 egg yolks

⅓ cup packed brown sugar

1 tablespoon unsweetened cocoa powder

1 teaspoon vanilla

¼ teaspoon salt

1¼ cups water

1. Heat cream to a simmer in medium saucepan over medium heat. Remove from heat. Add chocolate; stir until chocolate is melted and mixture is smooth.

2. Whisk egg yolks, brown sugar, cocoa, vanilla and salt in large bowl until well blended. Slowly add warm chocolate mixture, whisking constantly until blended. Strain into 6- to 7-inch (1½-quart) soufflé dish or round baking dish that fits inside Instant Pot®. Cover dish tightly with foil.

3. Pour water into pot. Place soufflé dish on rack; lower rack into pot.

4. Secure lid and move pressure release valve to Sealing position. Press Manual; cook at low pressure 22 minutes.

5. When cooking is complete, use natural release for 5 minutes, then release remaining pressure.

6. Remove soufflé dish from pot. Remove foil; cool to room temperature. Cover and refrigerate at least 3 hours or up to 2 days.

MAKES 6 SERVINGS

PUMPKIN CUSTARD

3 eggs

1 can (15 ounces) solid-pack pumpkin

1 can (14 ounces) sweetened condensed milk (not evaporated milk)

1 teaspoon ground cinnamon, plus additional for garnish

1 teaspoon finely chopped candied ginger *or* ½ teaspoon ground ginger

¼ teaspoon ground cloves

⅛ teaspoon salt

1 cup water

Whipped cream (optional)

1. Whisk eggs in medium bowl. Add pumpkin, sweetened condensed milk, 1 teaspoon cinnamon, ginger, cloves and salt; whisk until well blended and smooth. Pour into six 6-ounce ramekins or custard cups. Cover each ramekin tightly with foil.

2. Pour water into Instant Pot®; place rack in pot. Arrange ramekins on rack, stacking as necessary.

3. Secure lid and move pressure release valve to Sealing position. Press Manual; cook at high pressure 8 minutes.

4. When cooking is complete, use natural release.

5. Remove ramekins from pot. Remove foil; cool to room temperature. Refrigerate until chilled. Garnish with whipped cream and additional cinnamon.

MAKES 6 SERVINGS

CINNAMON RAISIN BREAD PUDDING

4 to 5 cups cubed
    day-old French bread
    (1-inch cubes)

1 cup raisins

2 cups milk

2 eggs

1 egg yolk

¼ cup sugar

⅛ teaspoon ground
    cinnamon

⅛ teaspoon ground nutmeg

1¼ cups water

    Vanilla Rum Sauce
    (recipe follows, optional)

1. Spray 1½-quart soufflé dish or round baking dish that fits inside Instant Pot® with nonstick cooking spray. Combine bread cubes and raisins in prepared dish; toss to distribute raisins evenly.

2. Whisk milk, eggs, egg yolk, sugar, cinnamon and nutmeg in medium bowl until well blended. Pour over bread mixture; press bread down into liquid. Cover dish tightly with foil; let stand 15 minutes.

3. Pour water into pot. Place soufflé dish on rack; lower rack into pot.

4. Secure lid and move pressure release valve to Sealing position. Press Manual; cook at high pressure 35 minutes. Meanwhile, prepare Vanilla Rum Sauce, if desired.

5. When cooking is complete, use natural release for 10 minutes, then release remaining pressure.

6. Remove soufflé dish from pot. Remove foil; serve bread pudding warm with sauce.

MAKES 6 TO 8 SERVINGS

VANILLA RUM SAUCE: Beat 2 egg yolks and ¼ cup sugar in small bowl until light and fluffy. Heat 1 cup whipping cream to a simmer in medium saucepan over medium-high heat. Slowly add egg yolk mixture, whisking constantly 2 minutes. Remove from heat; strain into medium bowl. Stir in 2 tablespoons dark rum or brandy and ¼ teaspoon vanilla. Serve warm or at room temperature. Makes about 1¼ cups.

CUSTARD BRÛLÉE

5 egg yolks

½ cup granulated sugar

¼ teaspoon salt

1 cup whipping cream

1 cup milk

1 teaspoon vanilla

¼ teaspoon ground cinnamon

Ground nutmeg (optional)

1¼ cups water

¼ cup packed brown sugar

1. Whisk egg yolks, granulated sugar and salt in medium bowl until blended. Add cream, milk and vanilla; whisk until well blended. Pour into 6- to 7-inch (1½-quart) soufflé dish or round casserole that fits inside Instant Pot®. Sprinkle with cinnamon and nutmeg, if desired. Cover dish tightly with foil.

2. Pour water into pot. Place soufflé dish on rack; lower rack into pot.

3. Secure lid and move pressure release valve to Sealing position. Press Manual; cook at high pressure 35 minutes.

4. When cooking is complete, press Cancel and use quick release.

5. Remove soufflé dish from pot. Remove foil; cool to room temperature. Cover and refrigerate 3 to 4 hours or until chilled.

6. Just before serving, preheat broiler. Sprinkle brown sugar evenly over top of custard. Broil 4 inches from heat 1 to 2 minutes or until sugar bubbles and browns.

MAKES 6 TO 8 SERVINGS

SOUTHERN SWEET POTATO CUSTARD

1 can (16 ounces) cut sweet potatoes, drained

1 can (12 ounces) evaporated milk, divided

½ cup packed brown sugar

2 eggs, lightly beaten

1 teaspoon ground cinnamon

½ teaspoon ground ginger

¼ teaspoon salt

1¼ cups water

Whipped cream

Ground nutmeg

1. Combine sweet potatoes and ¼ cup evaporated milk in food processor or blender; process until smooth. Add remaining milk, brown sugar, eggs, cinnamon, ginger and salt; process until well blended. Pour into 6- to 7-inch (1½-quart) soufflé dish or round baking dish that fits inside Instant Pot®. Cover dish tightly with foil.

2. Pour water into pot. Place soufflé dish on rack; lower rack into pot.

3. Secure lid and move pressure release valve to Sealing position. Press Manual; cook at high pressure 40 minutes.

4. When cooking is complete, use natural release for 10 minutes, then release remaining pressure. Uncover; let stand 30 minutes.

5. Remove soufflé dish from pot. Remove foil; cool 30 minutes. Top with whipped cream and nutmeg.

MAKES 4 SERVINGS

6 cups cubed brioche, egg bread or challah (1-inch cubes)

1½ tablespoons butter

2 large plums, pitted and cut into thin wedges

⅓ cup plus ½ tablespoon sugar, divided

3 eggs

¾ cup half-and-half

½ cup milk

½ teaspoon vanilla

¼ teaspoon salt

¼ teaspoon ground cinnamon

1¼ cups water

Whipping cream or vanilla ice cream (optional)

1. Preheat oven to 400°F. Spray 6- to 7-inch (1½-quart) soufflé dish or round baking dish that fits inside Instant Pot® with nonstick cooking spray.

2. Spread bread cubes in single layer on ungreased baking sheet. Bake 6 to 7 minutes or until lightly toasted, stirring halfway through baking time.

3. Meanwhile, melt butter in large skillet over medium-high heat. Add plums and ½ tablespoon sugar; cook 2 minutes or until plums are softened and release juices. Beat eggs in large bowl. Add half-and-half, milk, remaining ⅓ cup sugar, vanilla, salt and cinnamon; mix well. Add plums and toasted bread cubes; stir gently to coat. Pour into prepared soufflé dish. Cover dish tightly with foil.

4. Pour water into pot. Place soufflé dish on rack; lower rack into pot.

5. Secure lid and move pressure release valve to Sealing position. Press Manual; cook at high pressure 35 minutes. When cooking is complete, use natural release for 10 minutes, then release remaining pressure.

6. Remove soufflé dish from pot. Let stand, covered, 15 minutes. Remove foil; serve warm with cream, if desired.

MAKES 6 SERVINGS

BRIOCHE RUM CUSTARD

1¾ cups whipping cream

2 eggs

⅓ cup packed dark brown sugar

3 tablespoons light rum

1 teaspoon vanilla

¼ teaspoon salt

1 loaf (10 to 12 ounces) brioche bread or challah, torn into pieces

⅓ cup chopped pecans, divided

1¼ cups water

Caramel or butterscotch ice cream topping (optional)

1. Spray 6- to 7-inch (1½-quart) soufflé dish or round baking dish that fits inside Instant Pot® with nonstick cooking spray.

2. Whisk cream, eggs, brown sugar, rum, vanilla and salt in large bowl until well blended. Add brioche and half of pecans; stir until blended. Pour into prepared dish; sprinkle with remaining pecans. Cover dish tightly with foil.

3. Pour water into pot. Place soufflé dish on rack; lower rack into pot.

4. Secure lid and move pressure release valve to Sealing position. Press Manual; cook at high pressure 35 minutes.

5. When cooking is complete, use natural release for 10 minutes, then release remaining pressure.

6. Remove soufflé dish from pot. Remove foil; serve warm or at room temperature. Drizzle with caramel topping, if desired.

MAKES 4 TO 6 SERVINGS

SPICED CHOCOLATE BREAD PUDDING

1½ cups whipping cream

4 ounces unsweetened chocolate, coarsely chopped

2 eggs, beaten

½ cup sugar

1 teaspoon vanilla

¾ teaspoon ground cinnamon, plus additional for garnish

½ teaspoon ground allspice

⅛ teaspoon salt

3 cups cubed Hawaiian-style sweet bread, challah or brioche bread (½-inch cubes)

½ cup currants

1¼ cups water

Whipped cream (optional)

1. Spray 6- to 7-inch (1½-quart) soufflé dish or round baking dish that fits inside Instant Pot® with nonstick cooking spray. Heat cream to a simmer in medium saucepan over medium heat. Remove from heat. Add chocolate; stir until melted and smooth.

2. Beat eggs in large bowl. Add sugar, vanilla, ¾ teaspoon cinnamon, allspice and salt; mix well. Add chocolate mixture; stir until well blended. Add bread cubes and currants; stir gently to coat. Pour into prepared soufflé dish; smooth top. Cover dish tightly with foil.

3. Pour water into pot. Place soufflé dish on rack; lower rack into pot.

4. Secure lid and move pressure release valve to Sealing position. Press Manual; cook at high pressure 35 minutes.

5. When cooking is complete, use natural release for 10 minutes, then release remaining pressure.

6. Remove soufflé dish from pot. Remove foil; serve warm or at room temperature. Top with whipped cream and additional cinnamon, if desired.

MAKES 6 TO 8 SERVINGS

QUICK AND EASY KHEER (INDIAN RICE PUDDING)

3 cups whole milk

⅔ cup sugar

1 cup uncooked basmati rice, rinsed and drained

½ cup golden raisins

3 whole green cardamom pods *or* ¼ teaspoon ground cardamon

¼ teaspoon salt

Grated orange peel (optional)

Pistachio nuts (optional)

1. Combine milk and sugar in Instant Pot®; stir until sugar is dissolved. Add rice, raisins, cardamom and salt; mix well.

2. Secure lid and move pressure release valve to Sealing position. Press Manual; cook at high pressure 5 minutes.

3. When cooking is complete, use natural release for 10 minutes, then release remaining pressure.

4. Stir rice pudding well before serving. (Pudding will thicken upon standing.) Garnish with orange peel and pistachios.

MAKES 6 TO 8 SERVINGS

CHOCOLATE CHEESECAKE

22 chocolate crème-filled sandwich cookies

¼ cup (½ stick) butter, melted

¼ cup seedless raspberry jam

3 tablespoons whipping cream

1 teaspoon instant coffee granules or espresso powder (optional)

½ cup semisweet chocolate chips *or* 3 ounces chopped bittersweet chocolate

1½ packages (8 ounces each) cream cheese, softened

½ cup sugar

2 eggs

½ teaspoon vanilla

1¼ cups water

Whipped cream and fresh raspberries (optional)

1. Wrap outside of 7-inch springform pan with heavy-duty foil. Place cookies in food processor; process until finely ground. With motor running, drizzle in butter; process until well blended. Press mixture firmly onto bottom of prepared pan. Spread jam over crust. Refrigerate while preparing filling.

2. Heat cream and coffee granules, if desired, in small saucepan until bubbles form around edge of pan. Remove from heat; add chocolate and let stand 2 minutes. Stir until well blended and smooth. Cool slightly.

3. Beat cream cheese in large bowl with electric mixer at medium-high speed until smooth. Add sugar; beat until light and fluffy. Add eggs, one at a time, beating well after each addition. Add vanilla and melted chocolate mixture; beat at low speed just until blended. Spread in prepared crust. (Pan should not be filled higher than ½ inch from top.) Cover pan tightly foil.

4. Pour water into Instant Pot®. Place pan on rack; lower rack into pot. Secure lid and move pressure release valve to Sealing position. Press Manual; cook at high pressure 45 minutes.

5. When cooking is complete, press Cancel and use quick release. Remove pan from pot. Remove foil; cool 1 hour. Run thin knife around edge of cheesecake to loosen (do not remove side of pan). Refrigerate 2 to 3 hours or overnight.

6. Remove side of pan. Garnish with whipped cream and raspberries.

MAKES 8 SERVINGS

POACHED AUTUMN FRUIT

1 orange, peeled and halved

2½ to 3 cups water

½ cup dried cranberries

¼ cup sugar

2 tablespoons honey

1 teaspoon vanilla

1 whole cinnamon stick

2 Granny Smith apples, peeled and halved

2 Bartlett pears, peeled, peeled and quartered

Vanilla ice cream (optional)

1. Squeeze juice from orange halves into Instant Pot®; place orange halves in pot. Add 2½ cups water, cranberries, sugar, honey, vanilla and cinnamon stick; mix well. Add apples and pears; stir to coat. (Liquid should just cover fruit; if fruit is not covered, add additional water to cover.)

2. Secure lid and move pressure release valve to Sealing position. Press Manual; cook at high pressure 1 minute.

3. When cooking is complete, press Cancel and use quick release. Remove apples, pears and cranberries to plate with slotted spoon; let stand until cool enough to handle.

4. Meanwhile, press Sauté; cook about 10 minutes or until liquid is reduced by one third and thickens slightly. Discard orange halves and cinnamon stick. Pour liquid through fine-mesh strainer into medium bowl; return to pot.

5. Cut apple and pears into 1-inch pieces. Add to pot; stir gently to coat. Serve with ice cream, if desired.

MAKES 4 TO 6 SERVINGS

PEANUT BUTTER PUDDING

2 cups milk

2 eggs

⅓ cup creamy peanut butter

¼ cup packed brown sugar

¼ teaspoon vanilla

1 cup water

Shaved chocolate or shredded coconut (optional)

1. Spray six 3-ounce ramekins or custard cups with nonstick cooking spray. Combine milk, eggs, peanut butter, brown sugar and vanilla in blender; blend at high speed 1 minute. Pour into prepared ramekins. Cover each ramekin tightly with foil.

2. Pour water into Instant Pot®; place rack in pot. Arrange ramekins on rack, stacking as necessary.

3. Secure lid and move pressure release valve to Sealing position. Press Manual; cook at high pressure 8 minutes.

4. When cooking is complete, use natural release for 10 minutes, then release remaining pressure.

5. Remove ramekins from pot. Remove foil; cool to room temperature. Refrigerate until chilled. Garnish with shaved chocolate.

MAKES 6 SERVINGS

PUMPKIN BREAD PUDDING

1 cup whole milk

2 eggs

½ cup canned pumpkin

⅓ cup packed brown sugar

1 tablespoon butter, melted

1½ teaspoons ground cinnamon

1 teaspoon vanilla

¼ teaspoon salt

¼ teaspoon ground nutmeg

8 slices cinnamon raisin bread, torn into small pieces (about 4 cups)

1¼ cups water

Bourbon Caramel Sauce (recipe follows, optional)

1. Spray 6- to 7-inch (1½-quart) soufflé dish or round baking dish that fits inside Instant Pot® with nonstick cooking spray. Whisk milk, eggs, pumpkin, brown sugar, butter, cinnamon, vanilla, salt and nutmeg in large bowl until well blended. Add bread cubes; toss to coat. Pour into prepared dish; cover tightly with foil.

2. Pour water into pot. Place soufflé dish on rack; lower rack into pot.

3. Secure lid and move pressure release valve to Sealing position. Press Manual; cook at high pressure 40 minutes.

4. When cooking is complete, use natural release for 10 minutes, then release remaining pressure.

5. Remove soufflé dish from pot. Remove foil; cool 15 minutes. Meanwhile, prepare Bourbon Caramel Sauce, if desired. Serve bread pudding warm with sauce.

MAKES 4 SERVINGS

BOURBON CARAMEL SAUCE: Combine ¼ cup (½ stick) butter, ¼ cup packed brown sugar and ¼ cup whipping cream in small saucepan; bring to a boil over high heat, stirring frequently. Remove from heat; stir in 1 tablespoon bourbon.

WARM CHOCOLATE CAKES

½ cup (1 stick) butter, cut into small pieces

4 ounces bittersweet chocolate, chopped

½ teaspoon espresso powder or instant coffee granules

1 cup powdered sugar, plus additional for garnish

2 eggs

2 egg yolks

1 teaspoon vanilla

⅓ cup all-purpose flour

¼ teaspoon salt

1 cup water

1. Combine butter, chocolate and espresso powder in small saucepan; heat over very low heat until mixture is melted and smooth, stirring frequently. Whisk in 1 cup powdered sugar until well blended. Add eggs, egg yolks and vanilla; whisk until blended. Add flour and salt; whisk until blended. Divide batter among four 6-ounce ramekins or custard cups.

2. Pour water into Instant Pot®; place rack in pot. Arrange ramekins on rack, stacking as necessary.

3. Secure lid and move pressure release valve to Sealing position. Press Manual; cook at high pressure 9 minutes.

4. When cooking is complete, press Cancel and use quick release.

5. Remove ramekins from pot. Gently dab paper towel over tops of cakes to remove any condensation. Sprinkle with additional powdered sugar; serve warm.

MAKES 4 SERVINGS

SUPERFAST APPLESAUCE

2 pounds (about 4 medium) sweet apples (such as Fuji, Gala or Honeycrisp), peeled and cut into 1-inch pieces

2 pounds (about 4 medium) Granny Smith apples, peeled and cut into 1-inch pieces

⅓ cup water

2 to 4 tablespoons packed brown sugar

1 tablespoon lemon juice

1 teaspoon ground cinnamon

⅛ teaspoon salt

⅛ teaspoon ground nutmeg

⅛ teaspoon ground cloves

1. Combine apples, water, 2 tablespoons brown sugar, lemon juice, cinnamon, salt, nutmeg and cloves in Instant Pot®; mix well.

2. Secure lid and move pressure release valve to Sealing position. Press Manual; cook at high pressure 4 minutes.

3. When cooking is complete, press Cancel and use quick release.

4. Stir applesauce; taste for seasoning and add remaining 2 tablespoons brown sugar, if desired. If there is excess liquid in pot, press Sauté and cook 2 to 3 minutes or until liquid evaporates. Cool completely before serving.

MAKES 4 CUPS

CHOCOLATE ORANGE BREAD PUDDING

4 ounces cubed
French baguette
(about 4 cups)

¼ cup sugar

3 tablespoons
unsweetened
cocoa powder

1½ cups milk

3 eggs, lightly beaten

2 teaspoons grated
orange peel

1 teaspoon vanilla

¾ teaspoon ground
cinnamon

¼ teaspoon salt

1¼ cups water

¼ cup hot fudge
topping

Maraschino cherries
(optional)

1. Spray 6- to 7-inch (1½-quart) soufflé dish or round baking dish that fits inside Instant Pot® with nonstick cooking spray. Place bread cubes in prepared dish.

2. Combine sugar and cocoa in medium bowl; mix well. Whisk in milk, eggs, orange peel, vanilla, cinnamon and salt until well blended. Pour mixture evenly over bread cubes. Cover dish tightly with foil.

3. Pour water into pot. Place soufflé dish on rack; lower rack into pot.

4. Secure lid and move pressure release valve to Sealing position. Press Manual; cook at high pressure 30 minutes.

5. When cooking is complete, use natural release for 10 minutes, then release remaining pressure.

6. Remove soufflé dish from pot. Remove foil; cool 5 to 10 minutes. Serve warm with hot fudge topping; garnish with cherries.

MAKES 6 TO 8 SERVINGS

PUMPKIN CRÈME BRÛLÉE

½ cup plus 6 teaspoons sugar, divided

4 egg yolks

1½ cups whipping cream

½ cup canned pumpkin

¼ teaspoon salt

¼ teaspoon ground cinnamon

⅛ teaspoon ground ginger

⅛ teaspoon ground nutmeg

1 cup water

1. Whisk ½ cup sugar and egg yolks in medium bowl until well blended and slightly pale in color. Add cream, pumpkin, salt, cinnamon, ginger and nutmeg; whisk until well blended. Pour evenly into six 6-ounce ramekins or custard cups. Cover each ramekin tightly with foil.

2. Pour water into Instant Pot®; place rack in pot. Arrange ramekins on rack, stacking as necessary.

3. Secure lid and move pressure release valve to Sealing position. Press Manual; cook at high pressure 9 minutes.

4. When cooking is complete, use natural release for 10 minutes, then release remaining pressure. Remove ramekins from pot. Remove foil; cool to room temperature. Refrigerate 2 hours or until chilled.

5. Just before serving, preheat broiler. Place ramekins on baking sheet; sprinkle custards with remaining 6 teaspoons sugar. Broil 4 inches from heat 1 to 2 minutes or until sugar bubbles and browns.

MAKES 6 SERVINGS

FUDGY CHOCOLATE PUDDING CAKE

¾ cup plus ⅓ cup granulated sugar, divided

1 cup all-purpose flour

¼ cup plus 3 tablespoons unsweetened cocoa powder, divided

2 teaspoons baking powder

¼ teaspoon salt

½ cup milk

⅓ cup butter, melted

1 teaspoon vanilla

½ cup packed brown sugar

1 cup hot water

1¼ cups water

Ice cream (optional)

1. Spray 6- to 7-inch (1½-quart) soufflé dish or round baking dish that fits inside Instant Pot® with nonstick cooking spray.

2. Combine ¾ cup granulated sugar, flour, ¼ cup cocoa, baking powder and salt in medium bowl; mix well. Add milk, butter and vanilla; whisk until well blended. Spread batter in prepared soufflé dish; smooth top. Combine brown sugar, remaining ⅓ cup granulated sugar and 3 tablespoons cocoa in small bowl; mix well. Sprinkle evenly over batter. Pour 1 cup hot water over top. (Do not stir.)

3. Pour 1¼ cups water into pot. Place soufflé dish on rack; lower rack into pot.

4. Secure lid and move pressure release valve to Sealing position. Press Manual; cook at high pressure 40 minutes.

5. When cooking is complete, use natural release for 10 minutes, then release remaining pressure.

6. Remove soufflé dish from pot; let stand 10 minutes. Serve warm with ice cream, if desired.

MAKES 6 SERVINGS

PRESSURE COOKING TIMES

Meat	MINUTES UNDER PRESSURE	PRESSURE	RELEASE
Beef, Bone-in Short Ribs	35 to 45	High	Natural
Beef, Brisket	60 to 75	High	Natural
Beef, Ground	8	High	Natural
Beef, Roast (round, rump or shoulder)	60 to 70	High	Natural
Beef, Stew Meat	20 to 25	High	Natural or Quick
Lamb, Chops	5 to 10	High	Quick
Lamb, Leg or Shanks	35 to 40	High	Natural
Lamb, Stew Meat	12 to 15	High	Quick
Pork, Baby Back Ribs	25 to 30	High	Natural
Pork, Chops	7 to 10	High	Quick
Pork, Ground	5	High	Quick
Pork, Loin	15 to 25	High	Natural
Pork, Shoulder or Butt	45 to 60	High	Natural
Pork, Stew Meat	15 to 20	High	Quick

Poultry	MINUTES UNDER PRESSURE	PRESSURE	RELEASE
Chicken Breasts, Bone-in	7 to 10	High	Quick
Chicken Breasts, Boneless	5 to 8	High	Quick
Chicken Thigh, Bone-in	10 to 14	High	Natural
Chicken Thigh, Boneless	8 to 10	High	Natural

	MINUTES UNDER PRESSURE	PRESSURE	RELEASE
Chicken Wings	10 to 12	High	Quick
Chicken, Whole	22 to 26	High	Natural
Eggs, Hard-Cooked (3 to 12)	9	Low	Quick
Turkey Breast, Bone-in	25 to 30	High	Natural
Turkey Breast, Boneless	15 to 20	High	Natural
Turkey Legs	35 to 40	High	Natural
Turkey, Ground	8 to 10	High	Quick

Seafood

Seafood	MINUTES UNDER PRESSURE	PRESSURE	RELEASE
Cod	2 to 3	Low	Quick
Crab	2 to 3	Low	Quick
Halibut	6	Low	Quick
Mussels	1 to 2	Low	Quick
Salmon	4 to 5	Low	Quick
Scallops	1	Low	Quick
Shrimp	2 to 3	Low	Quick
Swordfish	4 to 5	Low	Quick
Tilapia	3	Low	Quick

Dried Beans and Legumes

Dried Beans and Legumes	UNSOAKED	SOAKED	PRESSURE	RELEASE
Black Beans	22 to 25	8 to 10	High	Natural
Black-Eyed Peas	9 to 11	3 to 5	High	Natural

Cannellini Beans	30 to 35	8 to 10	High	Natural
Chickpeas	35 to 40	18 to 22	High	Natural
Great Northern Beans	25 to 30	7 to 10	High	Natural
Kidney Beans	20 to 25	8 to 12	High	Natural
Lentils, Brown or Green	10 to 12	n/a	High	Natural
Lentils, Red or Yellow Split	1	n/a	High	Natural
Navy Beans	20 to 25	7 to 8	High	Natural
Pinto Beans	22 to 25	8 to 10	High	Natural
Split Peas	8 to 10	n/a	High	Natural

Grains

Grains	LIQUID PER CUP	MINUTES UNDER PRESSURE	PRESSURE	RELEASE
Barley, Pearled	2	18 to 22	High	Natural
Barley, Whole	2½	30 to 35	High	Natural
Bulgur	3	8	High	Natural
Farro	2	10 to 12	High	Natural
Grits, Medium	4	12 to 15	High	10 minute natural
Millet	1.5	1	High	Natural
Oats, Rolled	2	4 to 5	High	10 minute natural
Oats, Steel-Cut	3	10 to 13	High	10 minute natural
Quinoa	1½	1	High	10 minute natural
Polenta, Instant	3	5	High	5 minute natural
Rice, Arborio	2	6 to 7	High	Quick
Rice, Brown	1	22	High	10 minute natural
Rice, White Long Grain	1	4	High	10 minute natural

Vegetables

Vegetables	MINUTES UNDER PRESSURE	PRESSURE	RELEASE
Artichokes, Whole	9 to 12	High	Natural
Beets, Medium Whole	18 to 24	High	Quick
Brussels Sprouts, Whole	2 to 3	High	Quick
Cabbage, Sliced	3 to 5	High	Quick
Carrots, Sliced	2 to 4	High	Quick
Cauliflower, Florets	2 to 3	High	Quick
Cauliflower, Whole	3 to 5	High	Quick
Corn on the Cob	2 to 4	High	Quick
Eggplant	3 to 4	High	Quick
Fennel, Sliced	3 to 4	High	Quick
Green Beans	2 to 4	High	Quick
Kale	3	High	Quick
Leeks	3	High	Quick
Okra	3	High	Quick
Potatoes, Baby or Fingerling	6 to 10	High	Natural
Potatoes, New	7 to 9	High	Natural
Potatoes, 1-inch pieces	4 to 6	High	Quick
Potatoes, Sweet, 1-inch pieces	3	High	Quick
Potatoes, Sweet, Whole	8 to 12	High	Natural
Spinach	1	High	Quick
Squash, Acorn, Halved	7	High	Natural
Squash, Butternut, 1-inch pieces	4 to 6	High	Quick
Squash, Spaghetti, Halved	6 to 10	High	Natural
Tomatoes, cut into pieces for sauce	5	High	Natural

A

Ale'd Pork and Sauerkraut, 51

Apple-Cinnamon Breakfast Risotto, 141

Apples

Apple-Cinnamon Breakfast Risotto, 141

Applesauce Custard, 192

Apple Spice Bread Pudding, 189

Cider Pork and Onions, 48

Poached Autumn Fruit, 204

Pork Loin with Apples and Onions, 46

Superfast Applesauce, 208

Sweet and Sour Red Cabbage, 149

Applesauce Custard, 192

Apple Spice Bread Pudding, 189

Asian Kale and Chickpeas, 128

Asparagus-Parmesan Risotto, 129

Autumn Chicken and Vegetables, 70

B

Bacon

Bacon and Stout Short Ribs, 19

BBQ "Baked" Beans, 124

Bean and Pasta Soup, 113

Beef and Beet Borscht, 172

Cheese Grits with Chiles and Bacon, 108

Colcannon, 181

Easy Corn Chowder, 151

Frijoles Borrachos (Drunken Beans), 139

New England Fish Chowder, 90

Potato and Leek Soup, 162

Bacon *(continued)*

Savory Cod Stew, 102

Split Pea Soup, 121

Sweet and Sour Red Cabbage, 149

Tex-Mex Chili, 21

Tuscan Beef Stew, 22

Bacon and Stout Short Ribs, 19

Balsamic Green Beans with Almonds, 169

Barbecued Beef Sandwiches, 27

Barbecue Turkey Drumsticks, 79

Barley

Barley and Vegetable Risotto, 135

Barley with Currants and Pine Nuts, 130

Creamy Barley Risotto, 125

Fruity Whole-Grain Cereal, 105

Mushroom Barley Soup, 123

Barley and Vegetable Risotto, 135

Barley with Currants and Pine Nuts, 130

Basque Chicken with Peppers, 62

BBQ "Baked" Beans, 124

Bean and Pasta Soup, 113

Beans, Black

Beef Fajita Soup, 29

Black Bean Chili, 111

Cuban-Style Curried Turkey, 78

Four-Bean Chili Stew, 114

Quick Chicken and Bean Stew, 140

Sweet Potato and Black Bean Chili, 176

Three-Bean Chorizo Chili, 37

Beans, Cannellini

Minestrone alla Milanese, 119

Ribollita (Tuscan Bread Soup), 185

Beans, Cannellini *(continued)*

Speedy Minestrone, 175

White Beans and Tomatoes, 106

Beans, Great Northern

BBQ "Baked" Beans, 124

Chili Verde, 42

Four-Bean Chili Stew, 114

Pesto Rice and Beans, 110

Quick Chicken and Bean Stew, 140

Vegetable Bean Soup, 158

White Chicken Chili, 145

Beans, Green

Balsamic Green Beans with Almonds, 169

Creole-Spiced Pot Roast, 28

Minestrone alla Milanese, 119

Pesto Rice and Beans, 110

Spicy Asian Green Beans, 156

Thai Red Curry with Tofu, 180

Beans, Kidney

Chorizo Burritos, 50

Four-Bean Chili Stew, 114

Mole Chili, 34

Southwestern Corn and Beans, 166

Three-Bean Chorizo Chili, 37

Vegetarian Chili, 136

Beans, Navy

Bean and Pasta Soup, 113

Hearty White Bean Soup, 118

Simple Sloppy Joes, 23

Beans, Pinto

Beef Fajita Soup, 29

Frijoles Borrachos (Drunken Beans), 139

METRIC CONVERSION CHART

VOLUME MEASUREMENTS (dry)

1/8 teaspoon = 0.5 mL
1/4 teaspoon = 1 mL
1/2 teaspoon = 2 mL
3/4 teaspoon = 4 mL
1 teaspoon = 5 mL
1 tablespoon = 15 mL
2 tablespoons = 30 mL
1/4 cup = 60 mL
1/3 cup = 75 mL
1/2 cup = 125 mL
2/3 cup = 150 mL
3/4 cup = 175 mL
1 cup = 250 mL
2 cups = 1 pint = 500 mL
3 cups = 750 mL
4 cups = 1 quart = 1 L

VOLUME MEASUREMENTS (fluid)

1 fluid ounce (2 tablespoons) = 30 mL
4 fluid ounces (1/2 cup) = 125 mL
8 fluid ounces (1 cup) = 250 mL
12 fluid ounces (1 1/2 cups) = 375 mL
16 fluid ounces (2 cups) = 500 mL

WEIGHTS (mass)

1/2 ounce = 15 g
1 ounce = 30 g
3 ounces = 90 g
4 ounces = 120 g
8 ounces = 225 g
10 ounces = 285 g
12 ounces = 360 g
16 ounces = 1 pound = 450 g

DIMENSIONS

1/16 inch = 2 mm
1/8 inch = 3 mm
1/4 inch = 6 mm
1/2 inch = 1.5 cm
3/4 inch = 2 cm
1 inch = 2.5 cm

OVEN TEMPERATURES

250°F = 120°C
275°F = 140°C
300°F = 150°C
325°F = 160°C
350°F = 180°C
375°F = 190°C
400°F = 200°C
425°F = 220°C
450°F = 230°C

BAKING PAN SIZES

Utensil	Size in Inches/Quarts	Metric Volume	Size in Centimeters
Baking or Cake Pan (square or rectangular)	8×8×2	2 L	20×20×5
	9×9×2	2.5 L	23×23×5
	12×8×2	3 L	30×20×5
	13×9×2	3.5 L	33×23×5
Loaf Pan	8×4×3	1.5 L	20×10×7
	9×5×3	2 L	23×13×7
Round Layer Cake Pan	8×1½	1.2 L	20×4
	9×1½	1.5 L	23×4
Pie Plate	8×1¼	750 mL	20×3
	9×1¼	1 L	23×3
Baking Dish or Casserole	1 quart	1 L	—
	1½ quart	1.5 L	—
	2 quart	2 L	—